Through the Morgue Door

PENNSYLVANIA STUDIES IN HUMAN RIGHTS

Bert B. Lockwood, Series Editor

A complete list of books in the series is available from the publisher.

Colette Brull-Ulmann

and Jean-Christophe Portes

Translated by Anne Landau and Margaret Sinclair

Through the Morgue Door

One Woman's Story of Survival

and Saving Children

in German-Occupied Paris

PENN

UNIVERSITY OF PENNSYLVANIA PRESS

Philadelphia

First published in French as *Les enfants du dernier salut* by Éditions France loisirs, 2017.

English translation copyright © 2024 University of Pennsylvania Press

Published by
University of Pennsylvania Press
Philadelphia, Pennsylvania 19104-4112
www.upenn.edu/pennpress

Printed in the United States of America on acid-free paper
10 9 8 7 6 5 4 3 2 1

A catalogue record for this book is available from the Library of Congress.
Hardback ISBN 978-1-5128-2558-9
eBook ISBN 978-1-5128-2559-6

IN REMEMBRANCE OF CLAIRE HEYMAN

Contents

Introduction

Anne Landau

▪ Colette Brull-Ulmann enjoyed a remarkably long life; she died in 2021 at 101 years old. Of all those years, the one that most marked her, perhaps, was the one she spent as a fledgling physician in the Rothschild Hospital in Paris during the Nazi occupation, and as such it forms the focal point of her memoir. To understand Colette Brull-Ulmann, you have to understand the Rothschild Hospital as she experienced it, and for that some background is necessary.

The Rothschild Hospital, which still exists, was built by the French branch of the Rothschild family in the late nineteenth and early twentieth centuries, on a site in the twelfth arrondissement of Paris. The location was carefully chosen. It was in a poorer neighborhood, close to indigent, mostly immigrant Jews who were ill-served elsewhere, yet it treated people of all confessions and all services were free. The Rothschilds also established an orphanage and a hospice for the elderly, just a few steps away. During World War I, the family offered the hospital to the nation, to treat war casualties, thousands of them, as the First Auxiliary Hospital of Paris. Returning to its original status after the war, the hospital gained repute as one of the finest, with its excellent doctors, medical staff, and nursing school. Its social workers were so esteemed that prior to September 1939, they were supervising and training the social work staffs in virtually all Paris hospitals. Its maternity department was legendary: Jewish women of all backgrounds chose to have their babies there.

Then came the war. In May and June of 1940, France suffered a humiliating defeat: in just six weeks, ninety thousand soldiers were killed, two hundred thousand were wounded, and another 1,850,000 soldiers were made prisoners of war. Thousands of infantrymen and officers abandoned the uniform. Panicked French citizens from the north joined Belgian and Dutch refugees fleeing south. On June 11, Paris was declared an open city, and on June 14, when the Germans entered the capital, they found it almost deserted. More than two million Parisians had fled, even the elected government had cut and run. It is estimated that over eight million terrified, disillusioned men and women and children, wealthy and poor, from the very elderly to the very young, families in cars, on foot, on bicycles, on horseback, even in carts and wheelbarrows, took to the roads of France. The propaganda machine had kept assuring the French of certain victory. It was the sudden discovery of defeat that influenced this precipitous departure—a flight of such biblical proportions that it has been called "the exodus."

An armistice, signed on June 22, 1940, divided the country into zones: the North, or Occupied Zone, was under German rule, while the South, the Unoccupied Zone, would remain under French control. The government moved en masse to Vichy, France, and elected Marshal Philippe Pétain, hero of the Battle of Verdun, the leader of the newly designated French State. Pétain had an almost messianic hold on a fearful people who desperately trusted that he could return their lives to normalcy. He called for a program of national renewal through a return to conservative rural French values, as he blamed France's defeat on "outside" elements. He and his xenophobic and anti-Semitic cohorts were determined to eliminate from French society those who, they were convinced, had for decades weakened the moral structure of the Republic—Freemasons, Communists, foreigners, and Jews.

What set France apart from other occupied countries was the composition of the Jewish community. They were French Jews and foreign Jews, and aside from religion, they had little in common. Of the approximately 330,000 Jews in France in 1940, about 135,000 were citizens. The French Jews were highly successful, well-regarded professionals, fully assimilated into the national fabric. They were secular: French culture was their dominant lifestyle choice. They had fought France's wars—1870, 1914—and proudly wore France's medals. They referred to themselves as Israelites, and they never doubted that the Vichy government would protect them, despite what was happening in other German-occupied countries. France was, after all, the first European country formally to emancipate the Jews in 1791. The remaining 195,000 were refugees from czarist Russia and Eastern Europe in the late nineteenth and early twentieth centuries, or from Germany and Austria in the 1930s. Some, like Samuel Brull, Colette's father, had been naturalized; they were bourgeois, fully integrated, and considered themselves one hundred percent French. More often than not, however, immigrant Jews were poor, mostly tradesmen, many with communist or socialist leanings. In France, they felt they would be free of oppression, and a Yiddish saying, "Happy as God in France," expressed that hope. But memories of persecution were never absent. Citizen Jews might trust their government, but from their long history, immigrant Jews could not; they could easily foresee its collaboration with Nazi Germany. In the end, they were right. Vichy hunted down many more immigrant Jews than French Jews, and by war's end, some eighty thousand Jews of France had perished: one-third were French, and two-thirds were foreign. Eleven thousand were children.

Vichy almost immediately set about enacting anti-Jewish legislation and policies. It set up its own anti-Jewish agencies, confiscated Jewish property, and used its own police force to carry out massive roundups that began in May 1941. And although the public thought that Vichy was targeting foreign Jews, its laws applied to French Jews as well. The Germans were delighted to let the French do their dirty work. Vichy regulations were enforced in both zones, and the only conditions the Germans put on them was that they be consistent with their own anti-Jewish ordinances. The laws effectively stripped all the Jews of France of their civil rights and liberties, and gradually excluded them from the public space and public service.

Legislation in the medical field was especially harsh. Save for a very few exemptions, Jewish doctors found themselves progressively dismissed from all public hospitals, from teaching in medical schools, from participating in medical associations. One Vichy decree placed a quota of 3 percent on the number of Jewish students allowed to continue medical school, another placed a quota of 2 percent on the number of Jewish doctors allowed to practice medicine in the entire country. How did all this play out at the Rothschild Hospital? As a private institution, the Rothschild Hospital was able to hold its own exams to offer positions to interns like Colette (and her future husband, Jacques), who as a Jew was closed out of the state exams, slamming shut all possibility of a medical career. It also hired many doctors expelled from public hospitals; some of these younger ones, from immigrant families, were more inclined to play a role in the resistance inside the hospital and beyond. Over time, Rothschild was the only hospital in Paris where Jewish physicians were allowed to practice and where Jewish patients could go for treatment.

This is how Colette Brull-Ulmann, who had doggedly continued her studies through the first years of the war, was able to launch her medi-

cal career as a lowly intern at the Rothschild Hospital: all other place-
ments were closed to her. Her initial excitement at this real beginning
was soon dashed, as she discovered that in December 1941, two of the
hospital's fourteen pavilions had been requisitioned to treat prisoners
from Drancy, the detention camp for Jews hastily set up in an unfin-
ished public housing project just north of Paris. The conditions at
Drancy were appalling—forty to fifty people per room, concrete floors,
windows with no panes, straw to sleep on, lack of food, a trough to wash
oneself, few toilets. There was an infirmary, but space and supplies were
inadequate. Prisoners became ill, and the sickest were transferred to
Rothschild for proper care. Two pavilions quickly became three, pregnant internees were sent to the maternity pavilion, elderly patients were
transferred to the hospice and children to the orphanage following a
hospital stay. As time went on and more people were interned, the entire Rothschild complex became a prison. French police—not German—
guarded it, barbed wire surrounded it, doors and windows were
eventually barred, and severe punitive measures were adopted to prevent escapes. The incarcerated were both foreign and French, especially
after 1942 when the Nazis pressured Vichy to arrest all Jews, regardless
of origin. They shared wards with Jews who were still free and a few non-
Jewish, mostly Communist, Resistance fighters who had been tortured and sent there to recover. One can only wonder why such excellent
care was provided to people who were then returned to Drancy, loaded
on trains, and deported "to the East," to the fate that the world now
knows so well but was barely guessed at then.

A wide-eyed young witness to all this, Colette Brull-Ulmann does
not spare any of the details. Her increasing horror led her unhesitatingly
to resistance within the hospital, through the unnamed clandestine network run by Claire Heyman, the social worker to whom her memoir
is dedicated. Given Brull-Ulmann's eventual specialty in pediatrics, it

is no surprise that for her saving the lives of innocent children was paramount and the act of which she was most proud. This she and her colleagues did beneath the noses of Nazis and French police alike, at the grave risk of torture and deportation. The heroes were not only doctors, nurses, and social workers, they were lab technicians, pharmacists, administrators, receptionists, cooks, laundresses, boiler workers, electricians. Sometimes even policemen. Jews and non-Jews.

I first interviewed Colette Brull-Ulmann at her home in 2004, just after I had begun my own research on the Rothschild Hospital. She was eighty-four years old, sharp and outspoken, optimistic, accessible. A handsome woman with a compelling voice that commanded complete attention. On camera she told me everything she could remember about her time at Rothschild. She was eager to show me the place itself and met me there the next day, pointing out the older buildings and the entry on the rue Santerre, which have been preserved as a site of memory— un lieu de mémoire—with its courtyard, administrative pavilions, and the gate she mentions so often in her story. She paused in front of the commemorative plaques, sighed at some of the names of friends who had lost their lives. We then took the walking path and sat down in the rose garden; Brull-Ulmann seemed lost in thought. This is how she remembered it, so clearly, back in 1942: a series of small, mostly two-storied symmetrical red brick pavilions separated by gardens and green spaces. Large windows. A tunnel connecting every pavilion, facilitating escapes. The grounds were usually quiet: a few doctors in yellow-starred white jackets, sharing stories and a cigarette; a few nurses wheeling the elderly; patients taking fresh air in the garden; children laughing and playing. And then she leaned over as if to share a secret, "You have to remember . . . The morgue was over there, and then when you walked down the rue Santerre, there was a small door, and that was the small morgue door that opened when I'd leave with the children.

That's how it was." Her desire, need almost, to have me see her story was striking. She knew she was the last survivor, the last witness to the tragedy and the heroism that was Rothschild under German occupation.

To me, Rothschild is a microcosm of occupied Paris, and Brull-Ulmann's memoir a microcosm of Jewish life, such as it was, during that time. She hides nothing—the fears, the horrors, the hunger, the despair, but also the occasional fun moments snatched here and there among a small gang of twenty-somethings charged with an unimaginable weight of responsibility, and most of all, the sheer bravado and outright bravery that led them to rescue so many lives.

May their memory be eternal.

The Rothschild Hospital was liberated one day after Drancy, on August 19, 1944. The insurrection to free Paris had begun. There were a few skirmishes outside the walls and (in true Gallic spirit) a barricade had been erected, but inside the hospital there was neither bloodshed nor drama. A doctor from the Comité médical de la Résistance, working with the Forces Françaises de l'Intérieur (FFI), walked in, unimpeded. The few lingering French police did not interfere. The hospital was populated solely by Jews. Prisoners who had for months faked illnesses, tore off their casts and bandages, tossed them in the air, and walked out. At the same time, busloads of weak prisoners arrived from Drancy. The flags of the Allied armies and the flag of the Free French Forces were raised over the main entrance, just above where the French police had maintained their checkpoint. The Rothschild Hospital was the first liberated public space in Paris.

It has been reported that a few days later, when the Americans entered Paris, Jewish American soldiers filled the synagogues and Jewish American military doctors rushed to the Rothschild Hospital to help provide medical care. Later, when the full scope of the tragedy of the

Shoah was coming to light, Jewish American doctors flocked to Roth-schild in a show of solidarity.

■ Translators' note: Colette Brull-Ulmann's story is told in vivid yet elegant French. We have tried to mirror her choice of language.

Preface

This is not the work of a historian.

This is an account of a life, mine, based on very distant memories. Certain details have become blurred with the passage of time, but the essential thread is there. I have tried to talk about my own memories, what I witnessed. And though I was but a bit player in her network, I wish, above all, to pay tribute to that extraordinary person, Claire Heyman, in the name of all those she saved.

My wish is for people to know what she did, and that she be remembered for it. For she took uncountable risks in the pursuit of what matters most: reaching out to children and loving them.

1

December 1942

I have only to close my eyes to see it all again.

Paris was plunged into night—not just Paris, but the whole world, plunged into hatred and destruction. At least at that hour there were few passersby, and so much the better. The fewer the people on the streets, the less the chance of being noticed. I had unstitched the star sewn on my coat and was carrying the false papers that identified me as Colette Mosnier, supposedly Breton and Catholic. If I were stopped, it would be worse for me (far worse), but I had no other choice. Better not to think about it.

I could hear my heart beating as I walked down rue Santerre, hugging the wall that made up one side of a huge quadrangle. Behind it were just visible the roofs of some tall brick buildings. Farther down a gate opened into a small, paved courtyard, leading to an open entry porch.

The Rothschild Hospital.

From their post, a kind of concierge's loge, two duty cops watched me enter. The hospital was guarded night and day. With time we had all gotten to know one another. We waved. If they knew I had come without my star, and with false papers! If they knew I would not be leaving the same way, through the main entrance, which was under constant surveillance, but through the morgue door.

If they knew what I had come to do . . .

With night and my scarf helping to conceal the missing star, I smiled at them, then moved on, the sound of my steps echoing around me.

My heart was racing because I had no illusions: if these guards caught me, they would arrest me. And most assuredly, they would hand me over to other police who would be far less accommodating, perhaps even to the Gestapo, and I would be beaten and forced to tell them what I knew. And even if I knew very little—for I was only a minor player in this network, a little twenty-two-year-old intern—I would undoubtedly talk. I knew how they dealt with their prisoners: at the hospital, I had treated a Resistance fighter who had been handed over to the Gestapo. He was half dead, bleeding, and covered with bruises.

If I talked, the whole network could be blown. All those children fated for deportation would have no hope of being saved.

In that moment I shivered with fear, then quickly put this thought aside.

Beyond the entrance, the hospital grounds were dark and silent. I could barely make out the beautiful central lawn, with its two-story, red brick pavilions on each side. To muster my courage, I thought back to my arrival there, a little more than a year earlier.

My first position as an intern.

■ It was the realization of a dream, a triumph for me. By fourteen, I had still not attended any school. So when I announced to my mother that I wanted to become a doctor—a pediatrician—she looked at me wide-eyed.

"You mean that you want to work in a hospital? As a nurse?"

"No, not as a nurse. As a doctor. I want to care for children in the colonies."

"Care for children . . ."

By 1934, my family had lost everything and had taken refuge in Tunis. With nothing to do, I enrolled in a nurse training course with the Red Cross. From my first contact with a hospital, I knew this was for me. Everything delighted me—the cleanliness of the wards, the doctors and nurses in uniform. I could easily see myself in a clinic deep in the bush, saving children from life-threatening diseases, like Dr. Albert Schweitzer. Never for a moment did I dwell on obstacles that might stand in my way, but my family was more than happy to remind me of them.

"Come on, Colette, that's ridiculous," my mother would say, worried. "To be a doctor, you know very well you need the *baccalauréat*! And you've never even been to school."

"Well, I'll go!"

And so I went. I attended the *lycée,* I got my *bac*, I passed the entrance exams for the Faculté de Médecine. And now, I was an intern.

But under what circumstances!

Since the defeat of 1940 and Marshal Pétain's rise to power, the government had unleashed multiple discriminatory measures against us. It was forbidden to attend the movies or the theater or to sit with non-Jews in the *métro*, where we were consigned to the last carriage. Jews could no longer be employed as civil servants, heads of companies, lawyers, or doctors.

A quota for Jewish students was instituted. By a miracle, I was exempted because my father was a war veteran, and so I was able to continue my medical studies. A second miracle: I was selected to be an intern at the only hospital in the country where we still had the right to practice—the Rothschild Hospital.

When I arrived there a year earlier, I discovered something else. At Rothschild we took care of prisoners from Drancy and other camps. We operated on them, hospitalized them, delivered their babies.

Rothschild was a prison hospital, an annex to the disturbing *déportation*, the conditions of which we knew all too well because we worked inside the system: fifty or more people per railway car, no food, no water. The children, especially the youngest, had practically no chance of survival.

Yet sometimes those who were admitted to Rothschild never went back to Drancy, for within the hospital there operated an underground escape network.

■ On that evening, I knew that one of our young patients was not asleep. He had been awakened soon after he'd been put to bed. He was warned to stay silent, and under those circumstances, children understood and obeyed; they were already survivors, accustomed to fear, to silence, to flight. I didn't know anything about this kid, whether it was a boy or a girl. Maybe we'd already met, maybe not.

But none of that mattered.

As I walked alongside one of the administrative buildings, I was cold and shivering even with my scarf and little felt hat. I could see my breath with every step I took. The ground glistened with frost and so did the air. Hazy little halos formed around the few lamps that were still lit.

Claire Heyman was waiting for me in her office.

"Good, you're on time," she said, before picking up her coat.

We went out again. A short walk to the room where the child was waiting. We did not turn the lights on, and we moved carefully down the dark hallways. Only half-awake, the child, a boy, was pale, his eyes wide with fear. I could only imagine the infinite number of questions he dared not ask.

We walked quickly to the building that housed the morgue. The boy was next to me, the sound of his shoes loud—first on the floor, then on the stairs leading to the basement. In my mind, the whole hospital must have heard the echo of our steps, the shortness of our breath.

And my heart beat faster as we descended into the depths of the building.

Claire Heyman pushed open the morgue door and walked down a hallway, bypassing the room where bodies were stored. At its end, with the two of us at her heels, she gently pushed on the handle of another door.

This door was not locked as normally it would have been. Inwardly I gave a sigh of relief: it was all going according to plan. Outside, the street was dark, the air icy, almost foggy.

In her office, Claire Heyman had given me an address somewhere in Paris. To get there on foot would take me a good hour. Taking the métro was out of the question: too many identity checks.

"You have two hours before curfew," said Claire. "Is that enough?"

I nodded. In the darkness, I could hardly distinguish the features of her face. I knew that if we were caught, she would be in much graver danger than I, for she was the head of the escape network. Yet her voice betrayed not a trace of anxiety. Who would be suspicious of her, the Rothschild social worker, smiling, calm, with nothing untoward in her background?

We exchanged one last friendly glance, and then I ventured out into the icy streets. I clutched the child's hand. Was he an orphan? Were his parents prisoners at Drancy or had they already been deported? I knew nothing and I didn't really want to know.

The important thing was to get him out, away from this antechamber of deportation. So we walked at a brisk pace in almost total darkness, terrified at every corner of encountering a patrol of policemen or German soldiers.

The sparkling, frosty sidewalks stretched out before us. We fled deeper into the night, into this huge, sad, occupied city, without exchanging a word. At the end, there would be freedom for this child. One life spared. . . . Perhaps.

2

Before

I was born in 1920 in Paris into a family of Jewish immigrants from Romania on my father's side, and Jewish *pieds-noirs** on my mother's. My paternal grandfather, a dignified old man whose age, in the eyes of this little girl, seemed almost biblical (he died when I was eleven), never really talked about his coming to France.

He had very blue eyes, a long beard, and white hair, and every Sunday we visited him.

With him, the ritual was always the same. We children would call out: "Hello, Grandpa!"

"Hello, children!" he would reply.

And from his pocket he would produce a little box of flat, red hard candies called Coquelicots. We would religiously work our way through these "red poppies" while the grown-ups talked their grown-up talk.

My grandmother was a frail woman who seemed to me extraordinarily old (although she could not have been older than her husband). Very self-effacing, she took little part in these conversations because she was profoundly deaf. Her children (seven in all) took turns shouting in her ear to explain what was happening, so family conversations sometimes turned into bedlam. When I became a doctor, I realized she

*Term to describe French citizens of French North Africa.

suffered from otospongiosis, a bone disorder that causes deafness in women and worsens with every pregnancy.

Grandpa spoke perfect French, with a slight accent that made him roll his *r*'s. For him, the Promised Land was France, and he did everything he could to become part of it. He had left his native village in Romania (near the Moldavian border) to join his brother-in-law, a junk dealer named Horn, in Vincennes. At first he wanted to settle in the United States, but he was never able to assemble the funds necessary to move there with his family.

In Paris, Abraham Brull (later he called himself Albert) worked at his trade as a cabinetmaker and sculptor in wood in the Faubourg Saint-Antoine. He did that for thirty-five years and ended up a foreman.

He never talked about his past and made it a point of honor not to speak Yiddish in front of his children, to whom he gave strictly French names (at least to those born here): Isidore, Maurice, Renée, and Blanche. In the late 1880s, my grandfather became a citizen along with his wife and the two children born earlier in Romania.

My father, Samuel Brull, was a child of the Republic. Being from a poor immigrant family, he walked every day, whatever the weather, to the local school in the twelfth arrondissement of Paris, at the time a largely working-class neighborhood. His New Year's present was often an orange, with a barley sugar straw to suck the juice out of it. With the exception of my grandmother, the family was not observant, because Grandpa Abraham (or Albert) was a committed atheist.

Samuel was a brilliant student, and after elementary school he was able to continue on and get his baccalauréat thanks to a scholarship. (He ate better at the school canteen than at home; he especially enjoyed the fish, which the Brulls never cooked. One day he told me how disgusted he was with a dish he'd never seen before, skate wings in black butter sauce.) He then received another scholarship that enabled him to prepare for engineering studies and enter the École Centrale.

Today it seems very far away, but at that time France was dreaming of revenge. It wanted to wash away the humiliation of 1870, the debacle at Sedan and the annexation of Alsace-Lorraine. Our military had its eyes on the Blue Line of the Vosges Mountains—they were preparing for war. Nothing in the world would stop my father from performing his civic duty, so he signed up and spent three years under the flag as an artillery officer. Those three years would shape his future: despite his humble origins, he embraced the officer milieu and became cultured, passionate about music, painting, sculpture, and literature.

After the army, my father got a good job in the steel industry. He was the first Brull to earn a very good living, and he considered it his responsibility to help his brothers and sisters, who were born in France and therefore much younger.

He supervised the studies of Isidore (who later changed his name to Jacques), who wanted to become a dentist. I remember a day in 1940 when I couldn't understand the structure and function of the sphenoid, a bone at the base of the cranium, and my father showed me where I was going wrong; he hadn't forgotten the lessons he'd given his younger brother twenty years before. His other brother, Maurice, became an automotive engineer with his help. Renée studied English and humanities at the Sorbonne, but she suffered from a severe case of scoliosis. Papa paid for her doctors and stays at the hospital in Berck; in vain, because she became progressively hunchbacked. She found a job as executive secretary to one of his friends, who owned a factory. Finally, there was Blanche, nearly seventeen years younger than my father and with no academic leanings. A suitable match was made for her with a young man, and my father set him up in business.

As for Sophie, his older sister born in Romania, there wasn't much he could do for her by way of education. She was already married to a certain Monsieur Cohn, a civil servant (who would later play a considerable role in Papa's life, but I'll come back to that later).

Papa was like a second father to all the Brull children, a good Samaritan who paid the bills and the tuition fees and set things right when there were problems. His brothers and sisters called him "the old boy," the confirmed bachelor who loved art and literature and had a good job. No one ever imagined that one day he would marry and have a life of his own.

In 1914, my father was called back to the artillery. He was thirty-four years old.

He saw three years of combat and was wounded twice, but he never spoke about it. I am almost convinced that my mother did not know any more about it than we did. Reading through his papers after his death, I found a citation he received. At the front, they were being sprayed by a German machine-gun nest that had to be located. My father crossed enemy lines and captured an enemy soldier who talked. The next day, the machine guns were destroyed.

As for the rest of it, he was silent.

Only twice did he give us a hint about "the rest of it," and that's a bit of an overstatement. The first time was in 1939, when war was declared.

"When I think of everything we did to avoid this," he murmured.

He was sad but determined. *Everything he had done:* that was a horrifying world, death given and death received, fear and suffering. All this passed in a flash across his face, and I felt a shiver run through my whole body.

The second time was in 1943. We were living in Neuilly and the Allies were bombing the area. The apartment was tiny. We worked side by side, with papers spread out on the table in front of us. The light was dim. Far away, planes passed, then bombs burst, exploding one after the other, vibrating down to our guts. Everything shook, even the air, and I jumped with each blast.

He looked at me, calmly. "You know, poppet, you needn't get upset like that. When you can hear the shells coming, that means it's not serious."

I looked at him, wide-eyed. "Not serious?"

"What's serious is when you *don't* hear them coming. That, that's the end. Do you see what I mean? In the trenches, that's how it was."

The end . . . I understood all too well. So now I was still paralyzed, but all the same reassured when I could hear the chilling whistle of the bombs. He just went back to work.

What is certain is that the second time my father was wounded had completely unexpected consequences for his own life, and therefore for mine.

All of France supported the front and our soldiers. Even before the mutinies of 1917, it was well understood that keeping up a soldier's morale was essential, and that led to the creation of the "godmothers of war." Usually these were young women from good families who were put in touch with our fighting men, their "godsons of war." They wrote to them, sent them parcels with gifts and photos. Sometimes the godmothers even met their godsons when they were on leave.

Human nature being what it is, it happened that occasionally this correspondence between young women and lonely soldiers turned romantic. Mismatched marriages were a real risk.

This is where my mother comes in.

Whereas Grandfather Brull was a modest immigrant worker from the Faubourg Saint-Antoine, my maternal grandfather, Moïse Smadja, was a very wealthy man from the upper-middle-class Sephardim of Tunis (the Brulls were Ashkenazi).

Born in poverty in Oran, Algeria, my maternal grandfather made his fortune with his three brothers in the wheat trade in Tunisia. Eighteen years old in 1917, his daughter Aïda—whom everyone called Idette—was raised as a princess. She studied music and singing, had a German governess, and frequented the best circles of Tunisian society. When the question arose of her becoming a godmother of war, Grandpa Moïse, somewhat worried, voiced his concern to a civil servant he knew, one Monsieur Cohn.

"You know how it is," Grandpa said to him. "We've no idea whom she might meet. I don't want just anyone courting Idette for her fortune. And then . . . we are practicing Jews. I don't want a non-Jew. You work for the Ministry. Do you know someone you can recommend? Someone serious and trustworthy? You understand me, right?"

It didn't take Cohn long to reply (and for good reason).

"I have just the right man for you. My brother-in-law. He's an engineer, top-level. Captain in the artillery and he is Jewish."

"A practicing Jew?"

"He respects traditions . . . He's a very serious man, a confirmed old bachelor. Your daughter isn't even twenty, he's almost forty. He's not looking to get married, there's no danger, believe me."

The confirmed bachelor was my father; Cohn was none other than the husband of his older sister Sophie.

Delighted to have found the perfect candidate—a confirmed bachelor!—Moïse Smadja agreed to a correspondence between my two future parents, seemingly a very wise decision because not only were they both very reserved, they were also geographically far away from each other. It was the Germans who hurried things along. In

1916, my father was wounded for the second time and evacuated from the front. And he got permission to visit his godmother of war, in Tunisia.

I don't doubt it was love at first sight for them, but I never believed my mother when she claimed that the Smadja family was equally taken with him. To the contrary, I am sure they imagined for their princess quite another husband than this almost forty-year-old engineer, serious and cultivated, certainly, with a good career, but no fortune to his name. This led Moïse to take certain measures so that his daughter was married under the dowry system, meaning that my father had no rights to my mother's money. A lawyer managed her estate, badly as it turned out, for when the family needed money, in the 1930s, everything had mysteriously evaporated.

In addition to the considerable age difference between the future husband and wife, there was the question of culture. Yes, they were both Jewish, but he was essentially an atheist and she was a practicing Jew. She was a Sephardi in the Eastern tradition, while he was Ashkenazi in the Western tradition, characteristically marked by shame and withdrawal.

There were concerns on my father's side, too, from his brothers, and especially from his sister Renée. I have never known why.

Be that as it may, Samuel and Idette overcame every obstacle and were married in 1917. My father, wounded twice, never returned to the front. The army put him in charge of a large steel mill in Trignac, near Saint-Nazaire.* My older sister Georgette, whom we always called Yoyo, was born there.

---

*Maybe the Forges de Trignac, which were operational from 1890 to 1945.

At last the war ended in bitter rejoicing, leaving behind vast areas of devastation, two broken countries, disabled and maimed veterans, and armies of orphans.

Samuel and Idette then returned to Paris, where I came into the world in April 1920.

3

The Harp

My very first memory is of trees. Trees, their silhouettes marching across the sky, letting flickers of sunlight fall on my buggy. I recall this moment clearly, my sister is beside me, I must be two or three years old. Compared to the lives of my father and grandfathers, mine was a dream, in a bubble protected from the world.

I was born in an apartment on rue Descombres, in the seventeenth arrondissement of Paris, quite near the Porte Champerret. At the time it was still customary for some women to give birth at home. My father worked in industry; I didn't know exactly where, but it was in metallurgy and that allowed us to live rather comfortably.

He was of average height, broad-shouldered. Except near the end of his life—and when living in clandestinity forced him to—he always sported a beard and a mustache, and that is how I remember him. His hair turned white early on, but it remained thick and long, so much so that his workers nicknamed him "Christ." Very athletic, he fenced and rode horses; I remember he also played tennis.

He was a busy man, so we didn't see much of him. At work I imagine he was serious and respected, but at home he loved to kid around, making puns and playing tricks. One of our cousins, who was rather pretentious, boasted—enough to make us sick—that she was a great musician. That prompted him to play one of his tricks on her. One day, he led her to believe that there were people in high places talking about her performing in front of some *very important* people.

"People? What people?"

My father put on a serious face. "From what I've heard, maybe Élysée. But don't repeat that."

My cousin turned ashen. "Élysée Palace . . . oh, my goodness . . ."

My father said no more, as if he feared revealing a state secret. My cousin's imagination and vanity did the rest. For weeks she waited for a call from the President of the Republic. Regularly, she voiced her concern to my father because she'd heard nothing. He would frown as if in deep thought.

"I don't understand . . . And yet, that is what I heard . . . Be patient. I'm sure it will happen."

But of course, the call never came. We had a good laugh over that one.

My mother was a different kind of person altogether. I admired her enormously. She was very beautiful, quite tall, dark-haired, always very elegant. Two evenings each month, my parents attended the Opéra or the Opéra-Comique. I can still see her coming into my room to kiss me good night, dressed in a gold beaded gown that glimmered in the lamp's soft light. To my child's eyes, she was a goddess rising from the waves.

She kissed me, then left the room.

"*Maman*, she's the most beautiful woman in the world," I would say.

Yoyo, my big sister, would giggle in the darkness. Only eighteen months older than I, she was almost my twin, but already she saw things from a different perspective. "You're so silly, little Colette!"

Apart from that, Yoyo and I got along wonderfully—time and our very different paths did nothing to change that. In some ways we were wary around Maman; not that she was mean, but she had a way of losing her temper very quickly and very loudly, evidence perhaps of her Mediterranean background.

She could start yelling at the slightest annoyance. When that happened, my father would tease her in order to defuse the situation.

"Watch out!" he would say with a smile from behind his beard. "Here comes the shrew of Champerret again!"

At times that worked and she calmed down. At other times she yelled even louder.

Very conscious of her social position, Maman never wanted us to go to public school. And even though he owed his own success to the schools of the Republic, my father never opposed her on this—probably to keep her happy, or perhaps just to stay off her bad side.

I owe my education, therefore, not to a proper teacher but to Miss Henderson, an English governess whom I met when I was four years old. She came directly from Oxford, where my Aunt Renée (the hunchback) had studied. She had just ended a post as governess and was looking for a new position, and that is how my father took her into his service.

Miss Henderson was a stern person, a spinster of modest origin, but brought up very much according to the straitlaced principles of Victorian England: There was good on the one hand, and evil on the other; there were things that were done, and things that were not done. One's word of honor was sacred. And one never betrayed one's friends.

She was immensely cultivated. She knew everything about the history of her country. She filled us with stories real or imaginary, about Robin Hood and the legend of King Arthur, the Hundred Years' War, and the life of Queen Victoria. All this was in the language of Shakespeare, and so I have been able to speak English fluently since the age of five.

It was she who insisted to my parents that we learn to read and write, above all my sister, who was going on six. My father therefore found us a French teacher, Madame Leveau (her name, Mrs. Veal in English, made him laugh a lot, giving rise to endless puns). And so we set off, the three of us, to her apartment, on the number 7 bus line.

Miss Henderson sat us down in the bus, and we watched the streets go by, with those Parisian buildings that form the scenery of my life. Normally I was delighted to be going somewhere, but I sat there in a dramatic sulk, not only because my mother had yelled at me once again for not being properly dressed, but because I'd been told that I would not be taking lessons with Madame Leveau. Apparently I was too young.

Rightly or wrongly, I always felt that my mother paid more attention to Yoyo, that Yoyo was her favorite. It's true they looked like each other: Yoyo had the same fine features and she was always impeccably dressed. I was small and chubby, perpetually dirty and klutzy, with my clothes on the wrong way.

Miss Henderson also noticed this difference in treatment. She was bothered by it and it irritated her, but she could not do anything about it, of course. As soon as we were with her, she did everything she could to make up for it.

The bus stopped to take on a few passengers, then set off again with the clang of the bell.

"Don't attach too much importance to appearances," Miss Henderson told us suddenly as she eyed the new passengers who had just sat down. "That is not what matters."

A rather hefty woman plopped down with a sigh as big as she was. I listened, a little surprised, because I'm not the kind to hold grudges and I had already forgotten my mother's earlier reprimand.

"So what does matter?"

"What matters, children, is to be polite and work hard. And to do what is good in life. Do you understand?"

"Yes. But doing good, what does that mean?"

"Doing good means to help others, and not do to others what you would not want them to do to you. It means to be kind to others."

My sister and I looked at each other, without saying a word. We always drank in her words; she seemed so convinced, and suddenly we were as convinced as she was. She would never lie to us.

"You see, Colette, appearances don't matter. If you are not well dressed, that doesn't matter. What matters is that you are a kind little girl and that you are always content with things. It's nice for everyone, and that's what it means to do good. Do you understand?"

"And me, am I not kind?" Yoyo burst out.

"But of course you are," replied Miss Henderson, all of a sudden a little embarrassed. "Let's go, we're here."

And we climbed the flights of stairs to meet this famous Madame Leveau.

I remember her apartment being spacious and clean. A worktable dominated her dining room next to a magnificent Mirus stove covered in colored tiles; you could find them in most Parisian apartments at that time. Yoyo took a seat at the table. I sat on the rug, like a baby, though I was nearly five. To keep me occupied, the lady of the house gave me pencils and paper.

While I was scribbling away, I heard her begin the lesson. First up, the alphabet. "*B* and *A*, what sound does that make?" Madame Leveau asked my sister.

"*BA*!"

I was the one who answered, clearly and gleefully. Madame Leveau frowned, leaned toward me, then turned back to Yoyo with the next question:

"And *B* and *E*, what sound does that make?"

"*BE*!"

It was me again, quick as a wink. I had my revenge. I may not have had the gift of elegance, but I did have what it takes for school. Or should I say what passed for school. Owing to Miss Henderson, who took my side, I left the rug and colored pencils to sit at Madame Leveau's table for the next lessons.

However, I must not have completely forgiven her for making me sit on the rug like a baby, and I took my revenge a few days later. One afternoon while she was talking about her husband to Miss Henderson, I suddenly intruded into the conversation:

"Your husband is not Monsieur Leveau."

Madame Leveau looked at me not understanding, and Miss Henderson, too, even more annoyed because she guessed I wasn't going to leave it there.

"So, who is then, according to you?"

"Papa says that your husband is Monsieur Leboeuf."

Mr. Beef—another of my father's silly jokes that I was only repeating and which amused my teacher not a bit. Taken aback, she turned quite red, and Miss Henderson demanded that I apologize in a voice that cut like a knife.

Madame Leveau was not spiteful and we went on with our lessons. In no time at all, I learned to read and from that moment on I spent most of my time deep into books, any books.

Once I was immersed, nothing could get me out. One day, when we were in the country, I remember being terribly hungry.

I closed my book and went to the kitchen. "Are we having lunch?"

"Everyone has eaten. Colette, look what time it is," answered my mother, irritated. It was four in the afternoon.

"We called you, but you must have been lost in your book. So we left you alone."

This growing passion for reading ended up being a bone of contention between us and would soon come to thwart the secret ambitions my mother held for me.

■ My mother was passionate about music. She did have a beautiful voice, the voice of an opera singer, a career she undoubtedly could have pursued if she had really wanted to. Years later, my father told me she had auditioned for a highly regarded teacher in Paris.

"Your wife has an exceptional voice," the teacher told him after the tryout. "Furthermore, she's been well taught and hasn't developed any bad habits. If she were to work with me for three years, I could guarantee her an extraordinary career."

This teacher had trained a number of celebrated singers, both female and male; he was not a fraud. But my mother never studied with him. She was, at that moment, pregnant with me, and I also think that she never wanted to abandon her social life, her evenings out, the comforts of a well-ordered existence.

But there was regret and frustration born of this renouncement: she hadn't been able to become a great artist. Her two girls would do so instead.

One day she asked us, "What do you want to do when you grow up?" Neither Yoyo nor I had an answer.

She went on, "Well, I'll give you a choice. Either you take up music and I will do everything I can to turn you into great artists, or you will go to the local school, like the concierge's granddaughter."

The concierge's granddaughter was the only person we knew who attended this mysterious *local school*. As a result, we thought very poorly of the place. She was a grubby kid and poorly dressed; we looked down on her, being ourselves daughters of the bourgeoisie.

Every morning she walked to school, with snot in her nose, dragging her heavy satchel. Were all the pupils like that? Was it a sort of prison for children? In my mind it was a filthy place filled with insolent kids who would soil the clothes I already had so much trouble keeping clean. And I could just imagine the scolding I'd get from my mother when I returned home in the evening.

Yoyo cried, "I want to be a great artist!"

Me, too. I nodded my head with conviction.

Later on I often blamed my mother for this episode.

"But you *wanted* to study music," she would then say. "I asked you and you made the choice."

I retorted that I hadn't had a choice and that we didn't know what we were giving up.

Yoyo felt the same way I did, although she was a little less hard on our mother.

When I was six years old, we moved into a very big apartment on avenue de Villiers in the seventeenth arrondissement. This was because our musical endeavors were great consumers of space: every day my mother practiced singing and playing on a grand piano, my sister had her own piano, and I got the harp.

I was chained to it, so to speak, a prisoner of music theory and scales.

This cumbersome instrument was absolutely not my choice, but that of Madame Rousseau, wife of a well-known composer of that time, from whom I took piano lessons (reluctantly). My results on the keyboard were all the more mediocre as I had no desire to apply myself.

Madame Rousseau opened up about it to my mother.

"Madame Brull, a piano career is terribly competitive. Colette will never succeed."

"Even if she works at it?"

"She is too lazy. I think she should learn an instrument, shall we say, less competitive. She would probably have a better chance."

"Less competitive . . . And what do you suggest?"

"The harp. I know a very good teacher."

The harp was not *competitive*, and for good reason. This instrument is horribly more difficult than a piano, a monument with forty-eight strings and twenty-one pedal positions! I therefore became an unwilling harpist. Madame Benda was my new teacher. She played admirably and once a week I took lessons at her home. Bad luck followed me, for she immediately noticed the perfect shape of my hands: to play well, fingers must be thick and muscular. I was a chubby baby, and at six years old, my fingers were thick and muscular. Just my luck.

And try as I did to do nothing, the sounds I drew from my harp were apparently magnificent.

"She doesn't do anything," my mother lamented.

Madame Benda agreed. "No, it is true that she does not work a lot. But the sound is superb. If she practiced a bit more, it would be extraordinary!"

To get to extraordinary, I was pushed without pity. For six hours every day, I was made to pluck the strings of my harp and I also had to study solfège, music theory. (Yoyo was on the same schedule, but with the piano.) I can well imagine that with all this, the neighbors must have been delighted when we finally moved.

In reality I cheated as much as I was able to, thanks to my own little setup: an open book on a stool; I turned the pages and kept reading as I vaguely practiced my exercises. Heard from another room, this more or less succeeded until my little trick was finally found out.

When Madame Benda was told of this, she was overcome. Not only was the harp being deprived of a future great interpreter but what is more, she was losing a pupil.

"You have to forbid her to read," she decreed. "Then she will be forced to practice her scales."

"Stop her from reading? But she adores reading!"

"Very well, then! As long as she has not done her work, forbid her to read! She will be forced to get on with the music."

Back at home, I was shattered. How could I survive one hour of theory and six hours of practice a day without a book? A life of torture lay before me. To make things even clearer, my mother locked the cupboard where we kept our books.

A few days later, my father came to see me and looked at me with a solemn and mysterious look on his face.

"It seems that you are no longer allowed to read?"

I nodded. Soon came the tears, big ones, coursing warm down my cheeks, but I gritted my teeth.

"You're not allowed to read the books from your library. But you can always read the books in mine if you want to."

I didn't answer I was so stunned: his personal library was filled with very serious books, nothing that might interest a girl my age. But my rage to read was so strong—just like my spirit of contrariness. I dried my tears and Papa wrapped me in his strong and solid arms.

Now I devoured great amounts of paleontology, geology, works on mathematics and astronomy that I could hardly comprehend. I read all of Molière, all of Racine, Corneille, the fables of Florian, the philosophical works of Volnay. And I didn't forget my reading in English, from Dickens to Shakespeare, in the original. Little by little, I was becoming a walking encyclopedia.

I was unaware, obviously, that a few years later all this would serve me well.

A prisoner of my arpeggios and scales, I lived cut off from everything. In the early 1930s, while the world lived on the edge of a volcano, I knew nothing of the dangers bearing down on us. I did not even know I was Jewish; or rather, I did not understand the implications that could have.

Even the basic facts of life eluded me in a family where secrets and silence were the rule.

In 1925, Yoyo and I spent the summer in England in Sussex, where we met Miss Henderson's family. Her father, a retired railway worker, had in his garden a railway car we used as a playhouse. Upon our return to France, an amazing surprise awaited us: Maurice, our little brother. Our parents had said nothing. We examined him as if he were a foreign object, but I remember being infinitely curious about him. I loved him straightaway and watching him grow was like discovering a new world.

This cult of secrecy also extended to my father's occupation, about which I knew very little except that he held an important position—later I learned that he was the director of a steel works owned by a rich but anti-Semitic family, so much so that access to certain aspects of the business was off-limits to him. When I was eight, I learned that he had taken a new position at an even more important company.

For some time Maman had been getting upset more frequently. Maybe because of Maurice? And maybe because I was definitely not practicing the harp to which I had become enslaved. At thirteen, I was almost a young lady, but whenever I was compared to Yoyo, I never measured up. She was always more slender, more elegant, while I was still the short, plump, awkward brunette, as indifferent as ever to my appearance and always deep in a book as soon as I had the opportunity. Sometimes I caught bursts of conversations:

"Ah, yes, the older one, she's pretty, isn't she? But then, the young one . . . what a pity."

One summer we went to Italy. There Yoyo—in spite of our differences, we remained close, almost like twins—shared a curious thought with me.

"Have you seen Maman?" she said. "I am sure there's going to be a baby."

"You're kidding," I answered, completely naïve.

"No, I'm not, look at her tummy!"

She could be right. I suddenly noticed that our mother's tummy was remarkably round. And to think that I became a pediatrician! Yoyo might well be nearly fifteen, and I thirteen, we might well be women, but never did our mother tell us about those things.

Yoyo's suspicions were confirmed on our way home at customs when an agent discovered the new set of baby clothes in my parents' suitcase. She waved it like a trophy in front of my mother who was furious.

"So I thought you had nothing to declare. What about this, then?"

"I can't explain," retorted my mother, glaring back at her.

At the same time, she made her understand by meaningful glances in our direction that there were things that could not be said, important secrets to be withheld. The customs agent blushed when she realized her mistake.

"Oh! Excuse me, I understand . . ."

She closed the suitcase and waved us through, but this time Yoyo and I were sure we were right.

My little sister Bijou arrived in the world in 1933. Another source of wonderment.

In between harp and theory, I watched her attentively. Through our eyes we carried on private conversations. I loved watching her take her bottle, and soon my mother had no qualms about leaving her in my care. She was all chubby, with skin deliciously soft and plump, and her two wide eyes were filled with questions and laughter. I loved it when she took my forefinger and gripped it as tight as she could as if to speak to me. Soon I was on the lookout for her first words as if I were her mother. I watched her when she pulled herself up and plopped herself down, when she rolled on her side, puffing and struggling to reach for the toys I held out for her.

When she was just beginning to walk, we left to spend the summer in a beach house my parents owned in Langrunes-sur-Mer, in Calvados. For a while my life was peaceful: no harp to torture me, no piano, no music theory (or almost none anyway), only books to transport me far from the pure Normandy sky, far from the beaches and the dunes.

But at home, something was wrong. And this was not because of Yoyo, Maurice, Bijou, or me. I overheard some serious conversations and my father no longer joked so easily. Even more disturbing, mother rarely got irritated with us. As if she wanted to protect us or perhaps because her concerns were truly more serious. A few days later, our parents called us together as a family. They stood side by side, facing the four of us and looking very grave. Through the window I could see the sky slowly turn a darker blue.

My father spoke. "Children, I have something important to tell you. There has been a very serious crisis in the United States. A financial crisis, and that means that many families have gone bankrupt because of the stock exchange."

"Gone what?" Yoyo asked.

"Bankrupt. That means they've lost all their money. Everything they have is now worth nothing. And you also know, don't you, that the company I work for is dependent on the United States?"

Yoyo and I glanced at each other. Thanks to all the books I had read, I knew where the United States was . . . in North America. But the other words . . . Crisis, crash, stock exchange. . . . All that was a mystery to me.

"You know that I work in a factory with workers, right? Normally, I get money from my bosses to pay them. But because of the crisis, I no longer get the money. And since I still had to pay them, I paid them with my money, my own money, do you understand?"

He sighed, seeking some sign of encouragement from my mother. Then he looked back at us.

"I have been paying them for a year. Now I have nothing left."

"To pay the workers?"

"Yes. And I have nothing for me either. We have nothing left. We have lost our apartment on avenue de Villiers."

Yoyo and I looked at each other, stunned, incapable of the slightest reaction. The sky was falling on our heads.

"Lost? But what does that mean?"

"Normally, I have to pay some money every month, it's called rent. And I haven't paid the rent in a very long time."

"Because of the workers."

"That's right."

"And how long has that been?"

My mother straightened up, stung to the core as if the question had caused her physical pain.

"Come on, Colette. What does it matter?"

"But she has a right to know." My father sighed. "It's been a year. That's it. And the apartment has been repossessed, and that means we cannot live there anymore."

"So we'll live here instead? What about the music lessons?"

"No, we will not stay here. I have written to your grandmother in Tunis. I am sure she will be happy to take you in, you four and Maman. We'll see about the lessons later."

No more music lessons. Now that was big news, but I didn't react to it.

"Us four? . . . But . . . what about you?"

"I will stay in Paris. I have to find another job."

"And all four of us are going to Tunisia?"

My father nodded and gulped.

A long silence followed. We could hear the seagulls far off and the muffled breaking of the sea onto the sand. His voice flat, he said things were not all that bad, that he would certainly find a way to make a living. He had a profession, he knew people, everything would be all right, it would not last forever, the family would soon be reunited. And Tunis wasn't that far away, was it? We'd all see each other for the holidays. . . .

I felt my throat tighten. I had to leave Paris for a country that was not mine; we were to be separated. I didn't want to do this, but I understood I could do nothing about it. Events were stronger than I, irreversible and cruel.

My little rich girl universe was in tatters.

4

Bijou

To me Tunisia was a foreign land. The city, Tunis, was divided in two, the European part (where my mother's family lived) and the rest. When I first arrived, I was horrified to see poor, dirty children roaming the streets. From our window I could see that some of them spent the night outside, but no one seemed to mind.

Despite our predicament, the Smadjas welcomed us warmly. An uncle put us up in one of his apartments, not too far from the rest of the family, who occupied several flats in the same building, grandmother on the second floor, my Aunt Yvonne (my mother's sister) on the third.

She alone gave us a less than welcoming reception, as if we had brought some shame on her personally, as if she was adopting the same misgivings as Moïse, my grandfather, who had since died. Our pitiful arrival perhaps confirmed to her what he had thought: Samuel Brull, Romanian-born and naturalized and Ashkenazi on top of that, was a good-for-nothing, incapable of providing a decent life for his wife and four children.

I did not care for this woman and she did not care for me. She was married to a general practitioner, and I remember the curiosity I felt when I visited his office: the waiting room with all the patients and my uncle's examination room. People walked in anxious and left reassured. That made an impression on me, etched in my mind in spite of myself.

My mother soon resumed her old social life, but we children were excluded from it.

Little by little I grew accustomed to this new world, a form of exile really. It was all so different: the food, the expressions, the manners, and the habits. Papa had my harp sent by boat and for a while, I thought the Conservatory had caught up with me, with its hours of scales and theory, everything I detested. But my mother had changed. She, who had been so intransigent, left me alone as if my resistance had finally overcome her ambitions for me. The harp gathered dust in a corner of my room and I no longer touched it. She knew it but said nothing.

For her part, Yoyo landed on her feet in no time; she found a job at the Conservatory, where she taught classes in music theory and supervised piano practice. She started to make friends, but I knew no one and had nothing to do.

I just went around in circles.

I spent most of my time taking care of Bijou, my little sister, who was then two years old, and I was thirteen years older. My life was not sad, quite the contrary. Bijou was delicate. I washed her, dressed her, gave her her bottle. I was crazy about this. More and more I loved watching her live and grow. I loved trying to figure out what the matter was when she cried, if she was hungry or not. In her I saw the mystery of life itself, a beautiful mystery that I found infinite, unfathomable. It was at this moment that my love for children, my desire to help and take care of them, was awakened. This has never left me, not for one moment. It was the same during the war when children had to be plucked from savagery, and again later when I became a pediatrician.

My calling as a doctor came on me all at once.

Was this because of my little sister Bijou? Or because of my uncle, the doctor with his waiting room and spotless examination room, his instruments, and thick medical dictionaries? Or was it because of the class I took at a hospital in Tunis? I don't have the answer.

One day, one of my cousins suggested we both sign up for a training course organized by the Red Cross in a hospital in Tunis. The point was to learn how to bandage wounds and give other minor treatments.

This was my first contact with a hospital, and I knew at once that this profession was for me. I returned home, my mind made up, no turning back. With all the experience of a fourteen- year-old, I, a child normally so discreet, so obedient, so ordinary, announced that I was going to be a doctor.

I can still see the baffled look on my mother's face.

"You mean you want to work in a hospital? As a nurse?"

"No, not as a nurse. As a pediatrician."

Her astonishment moved up a notch, but to my relief, she did not seem angry.

"Take care of children . . . But Colette, what's gotten into you? What are you thinking? You've never even been to school. Still . . . a nurse, why not? But a doctor . . . and a pediatrician to boot . . ."

I was steadfast in my decision. I had felt at home in the hospital. I loved the white coats, the beds in rows and the instruments neatly set out, the tapping of heels on the white tiled floors, the smell of ether and other medical products. I loved it all. I would be useful, I would help people. I would care for other children like Bijou.

"I want to work in a clinic, in Africa. They need doctors there." My decision came as a great surprise, to say the least.

In amazement my grandmother said, "Come on, Colette, it's all very well to want to take care of little black children, but to become a doctor, you know you will need the baccalauréat!"

At the time, the bac was reserved for a small elite, maybe one child in ten. And girls were very much in the minority. In other words, my chances of success were slim.

"I know. Well, I'll get my bac!"

"You just cannot *get* the bac. You are fourteen and you've never been to school. How are you going to do it?"

I persisted, and then my Aunt Yvonne joined the fray. The traitor, she launched her attack on me.

"So it seems you want to take the bac?"

"Yes, I want to be a doctor."

She looked up at the ceiling, somewhere between despair and commiseration.

"You're kidding yourself. Raised *like that*, don't you realize that you're worthless, my poor girl? You cannot do it, you know nothing."

"I know things. And I will learn at the lycée."

"At the lycée . . ."

And so it went.

I wrote to my father. Since our separation he corresponded weekly with each of us, Yoyo, Maurice, and me.

He quickly wrote back and encouraged me: since his financial ruin, he had changed his mind—his girls should pursue an education, just like boys. If I wanted to become a doctor, if I had the abilities to do so, he would help me as much as he could. This acknowledgment bolstered my resolve. From the other side of the Mediterranean, I could still feel his eyes on me, his faith in me, which has always sustained me since.

And there's another thing, let's admit it.

All my life, I had been the funny, goofy, little brown-haired kid, always oddly dressed, not very good at sports, even less so on the harp.

"Ah! If she would only try . . ."

Always hidden behind Yoyo. For years, our mother dressed us identically, my big sister and me. Twins, one of us perfect, the other a poor copy. Colette, the lazy one, the dreamer, her nose in her books, her blouses always stained. It was a miracle that the two of us always got along so well.

It took a revolt on my sister's part for my mother to stop dressing us alike. Yoyo stood up for me, soon after our arrival in Tunis.

"But Maman, why do you always make us wear the same clothes? Colette is not the same size as me. Don't you see they don't suit her?"

"But . . ."

My mother was speechless and said nothing more about it. Our Tunisian exile had definitely changed a lot of things: we had gotten closer to what really mattered, to who we really were. Yet even with my own clothes now, I could still hear the words:

"Oh, yes, the older one, she's pretty, isn't she? But then, the little one . . . What a pity . . ."

And so it continued. Yoyo worked hard. She was conscientious, she had friends. She was even starting to earn a living. As for me? Nothing. I did not think of myself as pretty, and it seemed that no one appreciated me. They said I was lazy.

All right then, I would become a doctor.

I would study, no matter how hard it would be.

And I would succeed; that's a promise I made to myself at fifteen.

"So, young lady, you've never attended school?"

I said that no, I hadn't. My father had found an elderly lady, a retired teacher, whose job it was to determine my level of education. She looked me over as one might examine a rare object.

"Well then, you'll do a composition for me. Take this piece of paper and write about your holidays."

I found this idea stupid.

"My holidays? I have nothing to say about them. Can I not write a proper essay?"

I had just scored a point. I was not so dumb as to conflate a grade school composition with a true French essay. The old woman was a little surprised and gave me a classic text on which to comment. After reading it, a good hour later, she put the paper down and looked me straight in the eye.

"It's very good, Mademoiselle."

I took this to be the highest compliment she was capable of uttering. She immediately wrote to my father to tell him that I was exceptionally gifted and that I absolutely had to be encouraged to study.

My head was already filled with vast amounts of literature and knowledge: Dickens, Shakespeare, Molière, the philosophers, astronomy, mathematics, all those scholarly books that suddenly came back to me, in French or in impeccable English.

I embarked on my studies at top speed. Thanks to private lessons in French, Italian, and math, I soon entered the lycée, thwarting my Aunt Yvonne's sinister predictions. Suddenly my life lit up. I felt myself come alive once more. Every day I came across new books, lessons, courses, written tests, teacher assessments. I loved the smell of paper and ink, I loved the big courtyard, the windows, and the shade under the plane trees. I loved meeting people my own age, some of whom became friends.

Paradise!

At midday I'd have lunch with my grandmother, then go home and take care of Bijou, who continued to be in delicate health. Her diet had to be closely watched. She adored my stories, and I took advantage of this to get her to eat: one bite, one bit of a story. Not even when I had my own children did I tell so many stories!

Between study sessions I took her for walks. Over time the neighbors grew accustomed to seeing us pass by: the two sisters, Colette, fifteen, pushing her two-year-old sister Bijou in her buggy. I'd gaze into her eyes and never stop talking to her, she was a part of me, I was her little mother. Sometimes I'd meet Lucette, a friend who had a little brother the same age as Bijou. During the holidays the four of us would meet up and spend the afternoon together.

I worked hard to make up for lost time. Failing the bac was out of the question. Somewhere I had read that the children in Black Africa were miserable, that they suffered from malaria, sleeping sickness, encephalitis. In certain illustrated magazines, there were pictures of men dressed in white, greeting lines of half-naked children, bringing them vaccines and good health, pictures that were horribly paternalistic and complacent but commonplace at the time.

But these weeklies were not my only source of news.

Since I had begun school, I discovered life and the world as they really were, from newspaper headlines that caught my eye as I passed by the kiosks every morning. And they were not reassuring. Thanks to my new friends, I quickly realized that the financial crisis that had made us penniless was only a foretaste of what was coming. Tunisia was a bit of France and so here too there were murmurs of the forthcoming catastrophe.

Several times my father had mentioned the same rumors when we still lived on avenue de Villiers. Something was happening in Germany, something serious concerning Jews. But back then it all went over my head.

In Tunis it was different. My new friends belonged to the Jewish Scouts of France.* They talked about Hitler and the Nazis, and the danger they represented to us. There were some Zionists in our group. They said we should all leave for Palestine and found a state there.

"There are already colonies there. They're called kibbutzim, and women and men work there together as equals. The land belongs to everyone. And there, we'll be left in peace."

"So you want us all to grow chickpeas and milk cows? That's it, the future of the Jews?"

"The state of Israel is the future. No more pogroms, no more Hitler, no more massacres. A state for us alone. *Next year in Jerusalem*, how does that sound to you?"

"We've been waiting three thousand years. Can't we wait a little longer?"

Laughter or arguments. We'd meet for lemonade under the shade of the two-tone awning of a café near the lycée. In front of us paraded the motley crowds of Tunis, Arabs and French, the fragrance of spices floating in the air under a blazing sun.

Others disagreed on founding this country in the Middle East, and I rather sided with them.

"We already have a country, we're French. Why should we leave? And to start with, what can this Hitler do to us?"

"You'll see, he's a bastard."

"We'll see nothing of the kind. If the Germans as much as put a toe across the border, it will be 1918 all over again: we will crush them like bugs, and that will be the end of it!"

---

*The Jewish Scouts of France (Éclaireurs et Éclaireuses Israélites de France), the Jewish section of the Scouts of France, was dissolved in November 1941 by the Vichy government. Many of its members joined the French Resistance. They rescued and hid hundreds of Jewish children.

These stories filled me with passion and alarm but didn't for one moment distract me from my goal: I didn't hang out much in the cafés or on the beach. I passed my baccalauréat at eighteen.

Every summer of our separation, the whole family reassembled at our small vacation home in Langrunes, which by some miracle survived our financial disaster. My plans had not changed, but something was troubling me and I went to talk to my father about it.

"I've been thinking about my studies."

"I'm listening, Colette."

"If I start now, I'll need a year to get my *licence*, and after that, I'll have at least seven more to go."

"And so?"

"So I know it's going to cost you a lot. Seven years is a long time. Yoyo has found a job. It would be easy for me to get my *licence* in English; I speak it fluently. I could earn a living right away and I wouldn't cost you anything more."

My father examined his fingertips as he thought about what I had said. We had grown closer since I decided to become a student. I was eighteen, but I felt he now thought of me as an *adult*, almost his equal. As if he could see himself thirty-five years before, starting his own studies, with the same fierce determination.

"Listen, Colette, you want to be a doctor, right?"

I nodded.

"Even if you told me right now that you no longer wanted to, I wouldn't believe you. You've fought too much for that. Listen to me: as long as I am alive, I want you to be able to get on with whatever studies you want. Our responsibility is to enable you to achieve as much as you can. As for the rest, it's not for you to worry about."

Much later, long after his death, I found out that he too had been tempted to study medicine. But the course was long and his family too poor to support him; he preferred becoming an engineer. When I found myself alone in Paris with him, he admitted to some regrets regarding our music studies.

"Harp and music theory lessons," he said, "I thought it was natural, that it was good for you. I was born into a society where girls did not receive an education. So I thought . . . I let your mother go ahead. She thought she was doing the right thing, too, and for Yoyo she was right. For you it was not so clear. I know now that you have made the right decision: you need to have a profession and be able to earn a living yourself. When Bijou is older, she too will go to school. She too will have a career."

From that moment, I was perfectly assured I would reach my goal; now it was all up to me. To be accepted into the Faculté de Médecine, I needed the bac, of course, but I also needed a PCB—a certificate in physics, chemistry, and biology—which was taught in Paris.

And so in the autumn of 1938 I left Tunis for the capital. As the boat made its way out of the harbor, I thought about the past four years with no regrets.

Not for one moment could I guess how completely my life was about to be turned upside down.

5

Student

■ Once back in Paris, it felt like centuries since I'd left. While we were in Tunis, my father had struggled to find another job. Now he was working for the War Ministry in the armaments section. For a short time he lived with his mother, then moved into a low-rent apartment in the fourteenth arrondissement, avenue du Général-Maistre. It was in one of those well-known, red brick buildings that still stand alongside Paris's ring road, the boulevard Périphérique.

I thought I would move in with him, but he didn't want me to.

"You know, I am working away from home all the time. You'd be alone all week waiting for me to return. That's no good. You are young, you need to be around people."

"But where do you want me to live?"

"You'll have a good place, don't worry."

He rented me a small room at the Cité Universitaire in Paris, that complex of university residences recently built in the spirit of the pacifism that marked the period between the two wars. There were about twenty buildings that housed students from all over the world. All nations must live in harmony, it was thought. My room was in the Dutch Pavilion, a big, very square white building.

"You'll see," he said. "The Cité Universitaire has everything you need."

When my father was in Paris, I would have dinner with him before returning to my apartment. And we had lengthy discussions, speaking almost as equals. I felt that I was rediscovering him, or rather discovering someone I had not known before.

▉ In September when classes started, the radios and newspapers spoke of only one thing: Hitler wanted to seize the Sudetenland, the tiny German-speaking territories that had belonged to Czechoslovakia since 1919. Yielding to this claim meant agreeing to carve up one of our allies. But refusing risked war; part of the army had been mobilized just in case.

My father talked about this often, his expression grim, like country folk who see a storm coming before anyone else does, and no one wants to believe them because they are on a picnic and it's a beautiful afternoon.

"Already we've just let the *boches** take Austria. We cannot back away. That would be the beginning of the end."

And yet we did back away. In Munich, our diplomats and the British agreed to allow Hitler to go ahead in exchange for vague promises of peace. The French were divided after that; they were either pro-Munich or anti-Munich.

Among my friends, we were also divided, but our main feeling was relief.

In the evening I said to my father, "You see? There won't be a war after all."

"War, oh, we will get a war."

I was astonished because, honestly, Daladier and Chamberlain kept insisting that they had saved the peace. And my friends, some of whom were the age to be mobilized, would not be called up now. Surely having peace was important, wasn't it?

---

*Derisive term the Allies used for the Germans in World War I and World War II.

"No, war cannot be avoided," repeated my father. "And now it will happen under worse conditions."

"Everyone says that the peace was saved."

"Well, *everyone* is wrong. Colette, I am telling you, there will be a war and what's more, we are dishonored. We did not keep our word with our allies. We delivered Czechoslovakia to those bastards. Who will stand behind us now?"

A sudden silence filled the apartment. In my circle, he was the only person to hold this view and his reaction surprised me.

"You say that, but two years ago the Germans reoccupied the Ruhr. Everyone said that was the end of everything, but you know that nothing has changed."

In 1936, Hitler had reoccupied the Rhineland—that is, the border with France—something that in principle was forbidden by treaty. Our government barely reacted.

"On the contrary, Colette. That changes everything. The English forced us to accept the reoccupation of the Ruhr because they did not want to go to war. Well, we didn't want war either. But we should not have given in. Thanks to that, Hitler has become a god to the Germans. And Italy, our ally before this business of the Ruhr, has drawn closer to him. And now it's starting all over with Czechoslovakia. You and your friends, you believe that Herr Hitler got what he wanted and now it's over. But what you don't understand is that he will always want more, and he is very happy we have abandoned our allies. Who will be next?"

I no longer knew what to think. My father was a thoughtful man who had seen war and now worked at the War Ministry. In his daily life he was not a Cassandra, but an incurable optimist who believed in mankind and hard work.

And if he was right? Did he know things we didn't?

"Everyone believes the Germans are civilized people because they have Beethoven and Goethe. But I know what they are capable of. I know what they did in Lorraine in 1914. They massacred thousands of civilians just like that, for pleasure, to show they were the mightiest. They are no better than the people who carried out the pogroms in Romania and chased us out."

And so, little by little, Papa told me the story of his family. No more vague allusions like Grandpa Abraham had given us, but the whole truth, so that the scales would finally fall from my eyes.

It wasn't poverty that chased Abraham Brull out of Romania. Sculeni, his village, was half Romanian, half Jewish. One day, my grandparents were startled by screams and the sound of gunfire.

"A pogrom."

"Yes, a pogrom."

I shuddered in horror. Why were we never told? There is always this kind of taboo with the Ashkenazim; they get massacred and they're the ones who feel ashamed.

The murderers ran through the village, looking for Jews to kill, as many Jews as possible. One of them entered our house and tried to rape my grandmother.

"Your grandfather stabbed him," continued my father, a hard gleam in his eyes. "He was just a simple cabinetmaker. After that, they had no choice. They gathered a few of their things and fled through the woods."

I winced, imagining the horror of it. My grandfather and grandmother, both twenty years old, fleeing in winter, with no money, with three children, my father just a baby. One of the children died along the way of hunger and cold. They buried him. Their journey brought them to France.

"And now it's happening in Germany," said my father.

"But not to that extent."

He shook his head in sadness. He explained to me that since the Nazis took over, Jews had been forced to close their shops. Their assets were seized. Little by little, they were excluded from civil service and from liberal professions like medicine and law. They no longer had the right to marry non-Jews.

"The Nazis eased up a bit in 1936 when the Olympic Games were held in Berlin. With journalists present, they didn't want too much of that out in the open. But once the games were over, it started up again and got worse. They even scratched out the Jewish names on the war monuments to the dead. Can you believe that?"

I was terrified. He knew a lot more than my girlfriends in the Jewish Scouts, who first told me these stories.

That fall things did get worse. In November 1938 there was Kristallnacht, when the Nazis destroyed Jewish synagogues and shops, and Jews were beaten or incarcerated by the thousands in concentration camps. They fled Germany by the trainload. Many settled in France, but others continued on and sought exile in the United States or Palestine.

"But why did they do it? These people had done nothing to them. I don't understand."

"There is nothing to understand. Hitler blames the Jews for losing the war in 1918. It's ridiculous and it's wrong, but that's the way it is. You know, there are people who hate Jews everywhere, even in France."

"But not like that. Not to that extent."

He shook his head again and dived back into his memories.

"Don't believe that. When I was working in the steel industry, it was made clear to me that I would not be promoted because I was Jewish. That is why I left and took a job with Muller and Company. You know that at present I'm a lecturer at the École Centrale. Normally, with my qualifications, I should have a professorship, but that will never happen. The director is an anti-Semite."

"That's disgusting!"

"Of course it is, but that's the way it is. So, you see, you have to pay attention."

Pay attention. I did not know exactly what he meant. I did not even know what being Jewish meant. In my mind, there was no difference between me and the other students. What happened in Germany was horrible, but Germany wasn't France.

This could not happen to us.

■ While the world darkened and edged slowly toward the abyss, I was nineteen years old and assiduously attending classes at the Faculté des Sciences, across from the Jardin des Plantes. To enter medical school, I had to obtain a PCB certificate—physics, chemistry, and biology. I was not good at physics, so I worked flat out, straining my eyes.

I focused on my objective, went out rarely, and saw very few friends. Colette the shirker, Colette who hid as much as she could to avoid practicing her harp, that Colette existed no more. I was at war, a Spartan in training. Fortunately, I conversed more frequently with my father, sensing perhaps that these moments were precious and that we would not get them back. And I got the impression that he, too, was seeking to make up for lost time and tell me everything he had not told us, his children, either because he was working or we were in our Tunisian exile.

While I knew him as someone who loved jokes and puns, he now showed me another side of who he was, someone with no illusions regarding humanity in general, no doubt a vestige of what he had lived through during the Great War. But he also maintained that one should always help others without expecting anything in return, and always show gratitude to those who have helped you—and that that was the meaning of human dignity.

I was surprised to find that he harbored no class prejudices. One day, he took me with him to see one of his former workers who lived in a seedy shack in a Paris suburb. An old man in a misshapen cap and threadbare overalls let us in. Inside it was clean but cramped, stuffed to the ceiling with souvenirs from faraway places, Asian, it seemed to me. A treasure trove right in the middle of a slum. I learned that the fellow had lived for a long time in Indochina and was an astute connoisseur of the art of that region. My father, the factory manager, questioned him with great humility and the old workman talked to us for hours, telling us everything he knew about it.

I got my PCB at the end of the school year. We spent our holidays in Normandy with Maman, Bijou, and Maurice, who had traveled up from Tunis. I was relaxed, certain that the new term at the Faculté de Médecine would go without a hitch. If I worked hard, I would have everything I wanted. And then I would go to Africa and take care of children.

What could possibly prevent me?

It was a hot September in Paris in 1939. Maman, Maurice, and Bijou had gone back to Tunisia, and I was starting a new year. One morning the air felt electric. I saw a man running, then diving into a shop. Housewives gathered, all speaking loudly. A crowd formed farther down around a newspaper kiosk. Kids were craning their necks to see what was happening, adults were fighting over the latest edition.

And as in a dream, I heard the words. I walked closer and saw the headlines spread out before my eyes, unreal.

Germany had just invaded Poland. An ultimatum.

Declaration of war.

I could feel my temples throbbing and the whole universe shifting, like when Papa had announced we were ruined.

▪ An officer in the reserves, my father was mobilized with the rank of lieutenant colonel. Initially assigned to the War Ministry in Paris, he soon disappeared for mysterious inspections that he never explained.

For a few weeks, we seemed suspended in time. I thought something would happen, but there was just nothing. France was at war, and that was that. Men were mobilized, I saw khaki uniforms everywhere, we were all given gas masks. We were organized and we were strong.

And I went on with my studies as if nothing was wrong.

Maman decided to return to Paris. The family, she declared, must stay together. I was really looking forward to their return. One day, I pushed open the door and there was Maurice, and most especially my darling Bijou. We fell into each other's arms, in tears. Only Yoyo, who was by now twenty and taught piano at the lycée in Tunis, stayed behind, on the other side of the Mediterranean.

Winter soon was upon us, the coldest in twenty-five years. In the cinemas, newsreels showed our brave lads struggling in the snow to bring fresh supplies to the front, reinforcing our Maginot Line, examining the wreckage of downed German planes. Public notices proclaimed: WE WILL VANQUISH BECAUSE WE ARE THE STRONGEST. But aside from Maurice Chevalier touring for the troops, nothing was happening, except for some vague skirmishes on the distant front, anecdotes blown so out of proportion as to be ridiculous and boastful, as we would later find out. Maybe Hitler was afraid to attack us. He had crushed Poland, agreed, but France was something else.

Hadn't France won the last war?

My father was not of the same opinion, not at all. Between tours of inspection, he did not hide his pessimism.

"This is not normal. General Headquarters is not on top of things."

"Papa, you mustn't say that! What do you expect them to do?"

"They shouldn't leave us like this, doing nothing. We are losing the war. In 1939, Hitler was taken up with Poland. That's when we should have attacked. Instead, we've been quietly waiting around. Waiting for what?"

■ In the spring of 1940, we learned on the radio that the Wehrmacht was attacking in the Ardennes (the border that our highly decorated military strategists had thought unnecessary to fortify). Terrifying news, despite the propaganda machine in full throttle, insisting that it was nothing, that everything would work out fine. Still it was hard to swallow. For nearly eight months we'd heard time and again that the Germans were afraid, badly equipped, and poorly commanded. So how was this surprise offensive possible? Especially since it did not really seem to have been stopped.

Days passed.

We counterattacked in Belgium. The Germans continued their charge toward the sea. No one understood anything. A sinking feeling set in, like when you suddenly realize you've been the victim of a huge swindle. At first you are unaware of it, then you tell yourself there is nothing to it, and then the proof starts pouring in, whipping you in the face. A few days later we found out that, along with the British, most of our troops had been driven to the coast and cornered. This was at Dunkirk, on the North Sea. There had to be an emergency evacuation to England.

The radio kept lying to us, stubbornly, stupidly. They said that General Headquarters had anticipated a *strategic withdrawal*, a *flexible defense*. It had been planned in advance, it would all work out.

It all worked out so well that a few days later, we watched, incredulous, as the first refugees arrived. Their features were sunken, they were exhausted, stunned by the heat. Old people, children, mattresses and valises piled on top of one another in their carts. They were hungry and thirsty in the midst of a June heat wave. They didn't stop in Paris but continued on south, and their terror was contagious.

Barely had we digested the shock of Dunkirk when we learned that the Germans had launched another offensive. Where? One evening I found my father at the apartment. He had arrived unexpectedly, with a friend. He seemed very focused, more serious than usual.

"Ah, Colette! Hurry up and get your things together," he said, in a tone that brooked no reply. "You are leaving Paris."

I saw there were suitcases in the hallway, with clothes already piled on top of them. "Leaving Paris? What's happening?"

"What's happening is that the boches have launched another offensive, against Paris. The front will not hold; they will be here in a week."

"In a week? Here?"

"Maybe even sooner than that. According to what I've heard, Paris will be declared an open city. My friend here is taking you to Royan. He has a house there."

So Bijou, Maurice, Maman, and I set out in stunned silence. We watched the trees flicking by as we drove along the main road. We passed through silent villages where the inhabitants were themselves preparing to flee. How was such a disaster possible? Was this really happening? We overtook lines of people walking, wheelbarrows, carts, an occasional automobile. But very few soldiers, where were they? Our conversation turned to the bridges over the Loire. Our driver said that they might have been blown up. But no, they were intact, and we crossed the river. Two days later, we reached Royan.

It was a holiday town, filled with sunshine and teeming with people; women, children, and old people mingled together, strange summer vacationers with pale faces, searching endlessly for news or something to eat. The refugees haphazardly massed together as the municipality tried its best to feed them. We listened frantically to the radio. It appeared that we were fighting, but no one believed it. The roads were being bombed, the people of France were in flight, a shameful flight, aimless, filthy, starving, selfish. France was humiliated; I was so angry I could weep. And we were caught up in this miserable crowd.

The Germans advanced and advanced some more.

We stayed in a pretty seaside villa, parasol pines under a perfect cloudless sky, generous sunshine, the pure ocean air, all of which we scarcely noticed. For we were living in a nightmare, where the scenery was made of cardboard and it was falling apart. The old country was disintegrating before our eyes.

A few days after we settled in, our father appeared suddenly, in uniform. He asked us how things were going, if there was anything we needed. His mood was somber, angry, curt. The man who never ever talked about anything unleashed on us, spilling out what he had just lived through, why he was beside himself.

"I was in Saintes with my men. The municipality tried to stop us from blowing up the ammunition dump. Can you imagine? We almost got ourselves lynched."

He went off again, still angry.

That was the end. A few days later, Pétain was appointed head of the government and asked for an armistice.

A week went by and Papa reappeared, dressed now like a tramp. After he rested, washed, and had something to eat, he described his peregrinations.

He had tried to keep fighting (but many towns wanted no more talk of combat). He was taken prisoner near Saint-Jean-d'Angély. Overwhelmed by their sheer number, the Germans had dumped them all in a meadow.

"We might be prisoners," my father said to his men. "But there are more than two hundred of us and only three guards. We don't have to stay here."

"All right, but why leave? Pétain said that the war is lost. It's over now; we're going home. This is not the time to take a bullet."

None of them wanted to budge. So my father took off the jacket of his uniform and his kepi, bundled them up, and calmly sauntered out of the camp, looking like a farmhand.

He was furious with Pétain.

"This guy is vile. He's a traitor. We should never have signed this armistice."

"Wait a minute," my mother risked interjecting. "What else could he do?"

"At this point, not much. You're right. It's too late now. But for God's sake, General Headquarters did not do its job. We had just as many planes and tanks as the boches, but where was common sense? The losses have been enormous. It was shameful to just give up like that. And now, because of this pompous old ass, half the French army are prisoners."

"We know you don't like him. But aren't you blaming him for everything?"

"Not at all! He's an old swine. He was the one who ordered the fighting to stop, even before the armistice was signed. No one made him do it. He should have been put out to pasture a long time ago. We should have listened to de Gaulle."

Charles de Gaulle, he told us, was an army general who had launched an appeal from London a few days earlier. He wanted to continue the fight. In the 1930s, he had started advocating a modern approach to tank warfare, but the old farts who ran the army wouldn't listen to him—except for Pétain, actually, who then ended up changing his mind. They dispersed our tanks and planes in small groups instead of massing them together like the Germans. And they believed in the protection of the Maginot Line, which cost us a fortune and in the end was totally useless.

My father then left again for a few days. Later I found out he had reached Bordeaux and had thought about getting to London. But he came back.

He refused to abandon us.

▨ The train back to Paris was dreadfully crowded.

It advanced at a snail's pace, as if to make us atone for the disaster. The heat was horrible, the atmosphere unreal. Legs, stomachs, suitcases, and bundles all piled up; panic-stricken housewives, some belligerent, others demoralized. Not a lot of men. At times, tongues wagged. It was all because of the Popular Front, paid holidays, Jews, teachers, Communists, Freemasons. The Marshal would get us out of this mess, this time for good.

The rest, the majority, maintained a defeated silence.

I watched my father. He was impassive but I could tell by the blackness in his eyes that he was beside himself. Pétain had said that *the spirit of pleasure* had prevailed over *the spirit of sacrifice*. An insult to all those who had fought and died, and there were so many of them, their bodies still warm. How dare he?

Under the glass roof of the Gare d'Austerlitz, the heat was stifling and the crowd horrendous. We found Paris disfigured. Everywhere there were directions and signs in German, military vehicles, streets decorated with swastikas, as in some horrible, nightmarish celebration. And yet the weather was wonderful. We saw our first soldiers strolling in their grey-green uniforms, cameras slung across their shoulders like tourists in a zoo. Posters invited *the abandoned people* to *trust in the German soldier*. One depicted a smiling Nazi carrying a child in his arms.

With everything my father had said about the boches, I wasn't ready to accept their gifts. Nor to accept them. They wandered around our streets, very much at ease, as if the war was really over for good. I was appalled. I caught Maurice's eye; he was pale with indignation.

My father's face was fixed, gray, stoic. We were all silent.

A nasty surprise awaited us at our apartment on avenue du Général-Maistre. The door was locked, but inside everything was in disarray, the cupboards were empty.

The concierge had seen us arrive and poked her nose in the door, flustered.

"Oh! You're back," she said. "I meant to tell you: you had food, and we had nothing. I took it. I didn't think that . . . Well, I thought you were gone for good."

The bitch knew very well we were Jewish and that Hitler hated the Jews. Some Jews—the wealthiest—had already fled Paris. My mother's smile was friendly, but cold. "Oh, that's quite all right, Madame Delatour.* You can replace them for us later."

Her tone was as polite as it was contemptuous, and Madame Delatour sensed it right away. She stammered that yes, of course she would replace everything. My father, who had made a short tour of inspection around the apartment, fired the parting shot.

"I see that many of my bronzes are missing. I'd like to have them back."

She swallowed and stood there, ashamed.

"Yes, yes, of course. I took them for safekeeping, you know. But I'll go get them for you."

---

*The name has been changed.

"Yes, indeed, Madame Delatour. Come back tomorrow."

The next day, she returned the bronzes, with a flood of explanations. Germans, thieves, the war, her duty as concierge. Then she left, her smock stretched tight over her large behind.

So now, on top of the Germans, we had another enemy.

6

Jacques

Shortly after my return to Paris, I received notification that the final exams for the first year of medical school would be held. Clearly, the wheels of administration had not ground to a halt. I failed them, but in my misfortune lay a stroke of luck: there had been so many students absent that the faculty made us take them over. This time I passed.

And now, almost twenty-one, here I was in my second year of studying medicine.

Considering my bad start, I should have been living a dream, at least in theory, but the world had turned hostile. The German occupation was a constant humiliation. Obligatory curfew from eleven at night to three in the morning, forced acceptance of German currency, clocks set to German time, priority given to German soldiers on public transport, administrative forms printed in German, imposition of days *without meat*. Once we got over the shock of all this, protests began but the tone quickly hardened. The death penalty for destroying official notices. Prison for demonstrating in cinemas during newsreels. Movie house lights were soon left on while the newsreels were running—too many jeers and whistles.

And that was for everyone, the French as well. One evening, our father gathered us all together.

"Pétain's government has just instituted a statute for Jews," he announced, his face dark.

"A statute?" asked Maurice. "What does that mean?"

"That means that Jews no longer have the right to be civil servants, serve in the military, be teachers or journalists. We no longer have the right to manage businesses. They want to reduce us to nothing. We are no longer French like the others."

We all looked at each other, devastated. How was this possible? Truly, could this be the law?

"And what about the hospital? And school?" asked Maman. "And what about you? You're a civil servant, you work in a ministry. Are they going to throw you out?"

My father smiled sourly.

"I was wounded twice and decorated. That gives me the right to keep my job. And for Colette at the hospital and Maurice at the lycée, my status protects you both."

With a lump in his throat, he explained that, at the same time, the statute also delivered the foreign Jews, hog-tied, to the Germans, including those who had fled the fascists in earlier years. They would be assembled in internment camps and the Nazis could do what they wanted with them.

"It's an absolute disgrace. An absolute disgrace. They've even abolished the law banning anti-Semitic propaganda. It's as if they're saying, 'And while we're at it, why not?'"

I felt as if I'd been slapped in the face, over and over. I was humiliated, irate.

And I thought back to the conversations I'd had with my friends in Tunis: "And anyway, what could he do to us, this Hitler?"

Now we had some idea.

The memory of these words now stood out in disturbing relief. Had we been so naïve?

Like cattle at market, we had to be registered with our local authorities. I was scandalized, I didn't want to do it, but Papa was adamant.

"But why register? What's the point of that?"

"It's the law, Colette. There is no point. I guess they just want to humiliate us."

"Well, as far as I am concerned, I don't see why we should go and be humiliated!"

"You may be right but let me tell you again that we have no choice. Everyone knows we are Jews. The concierge knows. She can't stand us and she'd be very happy to tell the police that we did not go to register. And she's not the only one. They all know, everyone I've worked for. At the École Centrale, they know. If they didn't, they wouldn't have found it so amusing to block my career. If I don't declare myself, I will be denounced. Don't delude yourself."

So Papa had come to the conclusion that he had no choice but to register because so many people knew him. Yet he advised his brothers and sisters not to do so.

When we showed up at the local police station, ten or more people were already in line. Everyone's eyes were downcast, even mine; I couldn't help it. I had the feeling I was being punished, pointed at. I who had thought I was like everyone else. Among the lot of us, we had nothing in common. There were rich and poor, recent arrivals from Romania or Poland, bourgeois. We kept hearing that we caused the war, we Jews. We caused it? Was it this fat well-dressed woman, or this wrinkled old workman? Was it Bijou? Or me, a twenty-year-old student?

It was absurd and revolting. In line I saw a classmate whose name was "Gentile." With a grim smile, he told me his name was Hebrew in origin and that it meant "stranger."

Strangers in our own country, that's what they wanted to turn us into.

Once I got to the office, I took out my identity card to show the officer. Without looking up, he rubber-stamped JUIVE on it, in big square letters. I folded it up and gulped. I heard other cards being stamped all around me, no one said much. I continued my administrative round of the station; they asked me my name, my address, if I had a *certificat d'études*.*

"No, I don't have one," I said, straightening up, all the more angry.

"All right," said the officer after a brief reflection. "So I'll put down 'illiterate.'"

It almost took my breath away, I was so surprised. Illiterate! Was he really that stupid or was this deliberate?

"I don't have the *certificat d'études*, but I do have my bac and I'm a second-year medical student."

I spoke rather quickly and quite loudly. I was on the verge of making a scene. If anyone was illiterate here, it certainly wasn't me. I was about to say so, but I held back. He glared at me like a stupid cow.

"Ah . . . Wait, I'll ask my boss. . . ."

The boss appeared a few seconds later. He looked me up and down and decreed that I was not illiterate. I left, my papers duly filled out and stamped, and staggeringly humiliated.

However much I tried, I could not understand what was happening to us. Why were we being blamed for the war? Who had decided we

*Diploma awarded at the end of elementary education in France, certifying that the student has acquired basic skills in writing, reading, mathematics, history, geography, and applied sciences. It was officially discontinued in 1989.

were different? And just how were we different? It was all so grotesque, absurd, barbaric!

My father saw things much more clearly. He kept repeating that it was all because of Pétain and his clique. Unlike so many veterans who venerated *le maréchal*, my father had no confidence in him.

Worse than that, he loathed him.

"That old fool, that old bastard. Victor at Verdun, my eye! The real victor at Verdun was Nivelle. Pétain, he was only in command for two months and he walks away with all the laurels. And now that we've lost the war, he has the nerve to say that the army wasn't prepared. But who's he fooling? He was part of the High Command, a minister. He wants scapegoats? He should look at himself, not the Jews!"

"You've already said that, Papa."

With an angry wave of the hand, he continued:

"You'll see I'm right. When he was ambassador to Spain, all he did with Franco was scheme against us."

"Even so, the British abandoned us. Look at Mers el-Kébir . . ."

In July 1940, the British had destroyed part of our fleet off the Algerian coast because they feared our ships would fall into Nazi hands. More than one thousand French sailors were killed.

"Colette, you don't know what you're talking about. Our fleet was intact. The British had to be sure that the ships would not be used against them. We should have let them take the fleet rather than resist like idiots. That's proof that Vichy will defend German interests over our own or over the interests of our former allies, our *true* allies. As if the boches were really going to respect us more for that! I'll tell you what I really think: Pétain is *happy.* He wanted this defeat. France, yes, he loves France, but only *his* France, when France is afraid and losing. And now he's using us, the Jews and the Communists, as scapegoats, like Hitler in Germany."

He closed his fist but stopped short of banging it on the table. Luckily no one could hear us. Almost all of France stood behind the Marshal, who promised to *regenerate* the country. The defeat, well, that was the fault of some mysterious domestic foe, and at the top of the list, the Jews, always the Jews, to the point of obsession.

"But believe me, Colette," concluded my father, "these people will not win. We will not allow ourselves to be pushed around."

A terrifying look of resolve fell across his face, steeled his posture, and thrilled me with hope.

So long as he was there, nothing would be lost.

◼ Discrimination rained down with the regularity of a metronome. The minute one decree was put in place, another humiliation, another kind of harassment was announced.

Fortunately, my studies took up most of my time. In 1941, I was in my second year of medical school. I could have decided to follow the curriculum to the end without ever going near a patient, as some did, but these were not the best students. I was always thinking about those children I was going to care for in Africa. If I wanted to learn as much as I possibly could, I would need practical experience, and for that I needed to become an extern. This was the lowest level in the hospital hierarchy, but the best way to learn the art of clinical practice.

I scoured the hospitals in the area looking for replacement jobs; that was how everyone started. After one placement with a hospital in Bezons, I found another position in Paris at the hospital Hôtel-Dieu, under the great doctor Professor Halphen. Little did he know that less than a year later, he would be swept aside like dirt because he was a Jew. I had a long way to go before getting my diploma, but at least I was finally working at a hospital. It seemed that an eternity had gone by since I had left Tunis. I had become a different person. Every morning, I came out of the métro at the Ile de la Cité, in the heart of Paris. It was rare not to see soldiers in their grey-green uniforms outside Notre-Dame, calling out to one another, laughing, taking pictures. They were about the same age as me. I would disappear into the Hôtel-Dieu pretending not to see them, then make my way along the colonnades surrounding the hospital's grandiose, rectilinear gardens.

I put my things away and changed into a white coat. There were seven or eight of us on rounds. We made our way slowly between the beds of the large public wards and I took notes as we went. We were strictly forbidden from taking part in even the smallest medical procedure; we counted less than nurses. But at least I was on the other side of the fence.

And while I observed, I was also being observed. I just didn't know it.

I became aware of it one afternoon as we were collecting our things in the large central cloakroom. The lockers had all been broken into. My purse was missing, a disaster even though there was only enough money in it for a métro ticket and a modest meal.

"Is there something wrong, Mademoiselle?"

A young man approached me, another extern. He was about my age, medium height, and I immediately noticed a white streak adrift in his thick dark hair. He peered at me, somewhat ill at ease, as if he didn't know what to say. Whether it was because of the theft or the way he came up to me, a little abruptly, I suddenly felt a bit embarrassed.

"My stuff's been stolen too," he said to me.

Silence. Someone went to alert the security guard. With the restrictions everyone was starving, so it wasn't surprising there were so many thefts. Then someone asked me if I too had been robbed, and I replied halfheartedly.

"It's stupid. Now I have no more métro tickets."

"Well, I've got some. I'll give you one."

He rummaged in his pants pocket and produced a ticket, which he handed me with a flourish.

"Take it. I always have a few in my pocket. Just in case. Take it, please."

So I slowly took the ticket, and we both pulled our hands back at the same moment, as if we'd been burned. He kept staring at me with his dark eyes, as if asking a silent question. Would we see each other again? The security guard had just arrived, surveyed the disaster, the ransacked lockers, and wailed loudly, but we paid her not the slightest attention.

"I'll give it back to you tomorrow."

"My name is Jacques. Jacques Ulmann." I smiled.

"I think I've heard your name before. Thank you for the ticket."

I did give him back a ticket; he didn't protest.

Jacques was also Jewish. He was a little older than I and therefore further along in his studies, a formal extern whereas I was only a replacement. We arranged to meet between rounds. Now I was happier every time I entered the hospital and crossed the vast entrance with its colonnades. I knew he felt the same way. I'd see him break into a smile as soon as we caught sight of each other. But we dared not touch, not even our hands.

I told him about my family, my father, how I discovered my vocation in Tunisia, my lightning studies. He told me about his childhood in Paris, that his family was originally from Lorraine. His father was an artist, a painter, and his grandfather a renowned sculptor. But I sensed sadness within him. At times he seemed absent, lost in dark daydreams. Was it because of the war? Because of all the harassment we had to endure?

Then one day he confided in me, while we were sitting in a café before going to study in the medical school library.

"There is something you should know," he said, carefully watching for my response.

From his manner, I could tell he was still hesitant.

"You can tell me. I won't tell anyone."

"My father committed suicide." I turned pale.

"Suicide? But when . . ."

"In June. The day after the attack in Russia. He couldn't take it."

At the end of June 1941, the Germans had attacked the Soviet Union. Another thunderbolt that left us reeling. The first reports were alarming. Stalin's troops were splintered, the boches were moving on Moscow. They'd be there in a month or two. It was the end of everything.

Jacques held back his tears, a superhuman effort, and I trembled with sadness and compassion.

"That's terrible. I am so sorry, Jacques." He gave a wry smile.

"He was a patriot. He couldn't take it. Look, it's not your fault."

Hitler was crushing us under his heel. He'd taken Greece and Yugoslavia. He was destroying London with his bombs. And now he was going after Stalin. Would nothing ever stop him?

What if Jacques's father had been right? What if there really was no hope left?

After my experience as a replacement extern, I felt ready to tackle the exams to become an official one. I went to the office to register.

This had become my second home, the Faculté de Médecine. The great hall with its marble floor, its majestic staircases always crowded with people, the din of our footsteps, the comings and goings of students. I reached the office where I was supposed to apply. It was in a rather dark corridor teeming with candidates.

I came closer and saw the notice, I couldn't miss it.

The examination for the externat *is not open to Jews.*

A shock swept over me, red hot; I fought hard not to cry. Surely this was a dream, or rather a nightmare. I read it again, as students entering the office to register jostled me because I was in their way, standing in the middle of the corridor, frozen. I wasn't one of them. I would not be allowed to register. I'd be only a half-doctor. That is, if I was allowed to stay at the fac.

At home I told my family what had happened, shattered. Appalled. They were directly targeting me—my life and everything I wanted to accomplish. How absolutely unfair! My parents listened as I told my story, over and over, but they were powerless to help.

"I'm not Jewish, I'm French. French, like everyone else! I never go to synagogue, I don't know the prayers. We never observe the Sabbath. Who has the right to say I'm different from the others, to forbid me to study? What right do they have? What right?"

I sobbed like a baby and Papa eventually put his hand on my shoulder.

"It won't always be like that. You can continue school, can't you?"

"Yes, yes, of course."

"All right, you'll stay at school and you'll be a doctor. No one will stop you, believe me."

■ "Pétain hates Jews. It will end badly."

Jacques was even more pessimistic than my father. And bitter. He'd just been kicked out of the *externat*.

"Out with the Jews, out with the dirty Jews! That's what they were saying before the war—the fascists, Action Française, the Croix-de-Feu.* Now that they're in power, they're really enjoying themselves, the pigs."

Jacques was born in Paris, he had done all his studies here. Anti-Semitism, he knew it by heart, it had been going on for years, since the Dreyfus affair. Ancient history never forgotten, now resurfacing.

The broom swept through the entire medical profession and cleaned out professors, hospital doctors, and doctors in private practice, all reduced to a quota of no more than 2 percent. Foreign Jewish doctors were straight-out excluded from practicing. Even sick Jews were not allowed in hospitals. In principle, they had to find care in private institutions. (I say in principle because in reality many institutions did disregard this vile injunction.)

Jacques, too, was caught up in the storm: thrown out of the externat at Hôtel-Dieu. Overnight he had lost everything.

He told me the news in a café in the Latin Quarter we frequented from time to time. It was a splendid summer in Paris, and despite the restrictions, waiters in the cafés bustled around well-dressed gentlemen and ladies in flowered dresses. It felt strange sitting among all these people, we being pariahs. Two steps away, a German officer was sipping his beer. On his belt he carried his pistol in a black leather holster. From behind, I could see the curve of his closely shaven cheek.

I turned my eyes away and looked at Jacques. He had taken off his jacket and rolled up his shirtsleeves.

"So what are you going to do now?"

*Two French ultra right-wing, anti-Semitic, anti-Republican groups, early twentieth century.

I was curious to know and a bit anxious for him as well. He could leave, like some people had started to do.

"There may be a solution," he said after a long silence.

"Really? What is it?"

"You know the Rothschild Hospital?"

I detected a playful gleam in his dark eyes.

"A little, yes, I think it's north of Paris. Why?"

"It's in the twelfth arrondissement. The hospital was built by the Rothschilds, a Jewish family. They heard that all the Jewish interns and externs have been shown the door. So they're setting up a special exam, open to all. I'm going to take it. Maybe you should too, don't you think?"

"And they take Jews?"

"I just told you. They take everyone, even Jews."

"But the exam is for the *internat*. I'm not even at the extern level yet . . ."

"Don't be stupid. Of course you are. And if you want to, we can prepare for the exam together. You'll be qualified."

He smiled calmly, as if he was as sure of me as he was of himself.

"So what's your answer?"

My heart beat faster. I smiled back at him.

7

The Hospital

And so I became an intern. Jacques too. In normal times I should have been delighted but the fact is, it gave me very little satisfaction.

There I was, summoned to the Rothschild Hospital, in the heart of a working-class neighborhood I didn't know very well, with its grimy streets and buildings black with soot. As I made my way there, I could make out factories and workshops in the distance, much like the gritty areas just beyond the city proper.

I learned that the institution had been built at the end of the previous century by the extraordinarily wealthy Rothschild family. Initially they intended to accept only fellow Jews, who were often religious and very poor. But it became a neighborhood hospital, just like any Catholic institution that took in all comers regardless of faith.

With the new laws, the Rothschild Hospital was the last one in France where Jewish doctors were officially allowed to practice. For the beginning of my career, it was, I must say, quite special. I entered from rue Santerre, passing in front of a sort of concierge's loge where two uniformed policemen sat, watching me walk by as they watched everyone. We could see only their heads, but they carefully scrutinized visitors, especially those who were on their way out and whose names were checked against a list.

My heart was beating fast, a bit like my first day at school. I smiled to myself as I recalled my mother's face when, in Tunis, I told her what

I wanted to do. I remembered her doubts as well as those expressed by my Aunt Yvonne.

"That's ridiculous! You know perfectly well that to become a doctor you need the bac!"

That all seemed so old to me now. In seven years, if it all went well, I would be a pediatrician.

If all went well.

Beyond the entrance, I came upon the buildings, fourteen or so pavilions with mansard roofs. It looked more like an English college than a medical establishment. I passed nurses in white uniforms, their hair neatly tucked into their caps, doctors in long coats tied at the waist, wearing neckties or bowties. In the administrative office, I was told which pavilion I was assigned to and went back out, savoring for a moment the serenity of my surroundings.

"Ah! There you are!"

I turned around; it was Jacques. It was his first day, too. And I was happy knowing he was by my side, even though I would never dare tell him that.

He immediately confirmed what I suspected regarding the police. "The cops? They're here to keep watch on the patients."

I frowned. That was the first I had heard about police keeping watch on patients. "They're keeping watch? But what is there to keep watch on?"

"The Jewish prisoners. We take care of people from the camp at Drancy here."

"My father told me about that. In the apartment blocks that are being built."

"Yes, the low-cost housing. Not far from here. Actually it's not surprising they chose Rothschild to treat those patients."

I was quiet for a moment, thinking: what was the point of keeping all those people penned up in there? What had they done? What crime were they being punished for? As if he could guess what was in my mind, Jacques soberly went on:

"What are they going to do with all these people? No one knows. As if they didn't already have enough prisoners."

He stopped in mid-sentence, with a smile that wasn't much of one. The hunt for Jews had begun some months earlier. But only for foreign Jews. They were interned in Drancy, but also in other camps, in the Loiret or Compiègne.

"They are interned, but they still need care from time to time, don't they?"

"Yes, sure."

I certainly understood that. The camp infirmaries were most likely poorly equipped. But something I couldn't put my finger on made me quite uneasy.

"At first they were sent to Tenon Hospital," Jacques clarified as we strolled through the grounds, "but apparently there were too many escapes. Now they are putting them here. First, because it's a Jewish hospital. Then, with the pavilions, surveillance is much easier. And there's only one way in and one way out—through the main gate."

I learned later that he was wrong: you could also leave by the morgue door, and *that* way out saw a lot of use.

I was assigned to Pavilion Seven, which was general medicine, under Professor Paul Isch-Wall. The nurse who greeted me was about thirty years old, pint-size, blond, and round-faced, lively and smiling.

"I am Mademoiselle Damangout, your nurse supervisor. So you're the new intern?"

I said yes as she looked me up and down, favorably on the whole. Beneath her white cap, she was neither plain nor beautiful, but her affable country manner was immediately appealing. Instinctively, I felt I could count on her and my instinct turned out to be right; she may have had the manner of a busy housewife, but underneath it all, Mademoiselle Damangout was a woman of steel who was absolutely fearless.

She was one of the future combatants in the hospital's clandestine network.

For the moment she took me to her office to sign some papers. Then she gave me a tour of the hospital, which was much larger than I had imagined. There was a surgery pavilion, another for urology, the laboratory, an area for appointments in oral medicine, a maternity pavilion, and two pavilions for general medicine, one of which was mine. I also learned that there was a Rothschild orphanage, about two hundred meters away.*

Back in Pavilion Seven, my nurse supervisor showed me the women's floor, a big, very clean ward with a lot of natural light.

There was another floor for men that was exactly the same, but with one difference.

"Right now we have four sick internees."

Mademoiselle Damangout lowered her voice, as if it were a secret.

"They are allowed visitors, they can walk outside, but they cannot leave the grounds. I take it you must have noticed the policemen in their sentry box."

She quickly confirmed what Jacques had just told me. This was obviously upsetting to her, but what could anyone do? One of these prisoners—for that's what they were—seemed to me particularly young and tired. He looked at me, his expression was hard and dark, as if he were as wary of me as he was of his illness.

"We have quite a few surgical cases as well," she explained as she waved to me to follow her. "At Drancy, there is an infirmary, but there

---

*The Rothschild Orphanage, at 7 rue Lamblardie, was torn down at the end of the 1960s and replaced by a nursing home.

is no X-ray or surgery. They send us their serious cases and their emergencies, appendicitis, fractures, really all cases needing an operation."

She opened her mouth about to add something, then turned around and went on with the tour.

I said nothing, lost in my thoughts.

So this odd hospital was also a prison.

Still, I immediately felt at home. I liked some of my new colleagues and especially Mademoiselle Damangout. Always smiling, always on the move and efficient, she knew every patient and treated them all with kindness. She was the perfect supervisor, the linchpin of general medicine. She'd been working here for several years, and everyone called her Gougoutte (at least those who knew her well). To my surprise, I learned that she was not Jewish, like a good many on the staff. Cauvin, one of the new interns, was Protestant. A pharmacist, Pierre Dupont, was a staunch Catholic.

Jacques, whom I met at the end of the day in the garden, did not seem to share my enthusiasm.

"So, everything went OK for you?"

"For the best," he replied, with a tight smile. "We're interns, it's what we wanted, right?"

I sensed his bitterness and I shared it, too. It was true, we had played our cards right, we were continuing our studies in spite of everything, and we were learning our profession. But how could we feel good about it in a place like this?

With feigned enthusiasm, I told him about my meeting with Mademoiselle Damangout.

"I think we'll be all right here. It's a beautiful hospital."

"Maybe," Jacques replied.

He glanced at the entrance, and I could see his mind was on the police checkpoint. "It's strange how you can get used to anything, right?"

Since we had started at Rothschild, I saw more and more of Jacques.

Once or twice he took my arm when we were walking down the street, but it never went further than that. I may very well have had the most prudish mother in France, but I was in my second year of medical school, and I knew the risks we would be taking. Sometimes my thoughts wandered; I guessed we were close to taking other paths, other pleasures, but venturing there was out of the question.

My heart soared every time I saw him. I'd keep an eye out for his arrival. I loved looking at his black hair with the white streak, his slim silhouette; I loved his deadpan sense of humor and the sound of his voice, his jokes that were sometimes bitter, and most especially his dark eyes, which at times got lost in mine. I felt he was both solid and thoughtful, a serious person. I loved his gravity but also his lightheartedness.

We spent our time chatting away and laughing a lot, making fun of passersby, mocking the absurdity in the world. Yes, it was all bad and getting worse, but we weren't going to cry about it. What good would that do?

One day, he told me again about how he had spotted me among the externs when we were still at Hôtel-Dieu.

"Funny that you noticed me. I didn't notice you at all," I said, a little cheeky. He didn't bat an eye.

"But I was hesitant to speak to you. I thanked heaven the day that thief ransacked the cloakroom."

"Really? You could have spoken to me twenty times before that."

"I was waiting for the right moment," he answered, with an air of detachment. Without believing him, I smiled as I watched an elderly couple pass by.

We took lots of walks. Paris was very gray, bitterly cold. Often the only color around was the blood red of the Nazi flag. But walking along, side by side, we put it out of our minds. I was more talkative than he, and at times he seemed laconic, but we were never bored.

Sometimes we ducked into the movies and sat in the dark, wedged shoulder to shoulder. Everyone kept their coats on and sometimes we'd catch our breath rising in the light from the projector. We couldn't heat our houses anymore, so no one was going to heat the movie theaters either. Sometimes my hair brushed against his cheek, our fingers might touch on the armrest as we watched newsreels that made us bristle— German soldiers advancing on the Russian front within sight of Moscow; the Japanese destroying the US fleet at Pearl Harbor; winter relief for our prisoners in Germany;* Laval's and others' speeches on the Franco-German accord, against the Jews, the Communists, the Freemasons. Despite the lights being on there were still shouts and whistles: people were dying of hunger but they were not stupid. Those newsreels were all just an excuse to try to drum into us the permanent humiliation, the hunger, the looting, the contempt.

The winter of 1941 was horrible. We were cold everywhere and all the time.

There was no more coal, no more wood.

We had nothing much to give at Christmas and nothing much to celebrate. My father was earning a good living, but rationing was so severe and shops so empty that Maman could barely feed us. With Maurice, sixteen, and Bijou, eight, growing so quickly, she turned to the black market, the only place you could find the basics: butter, milk, meat, sugar, flour, and oil.

---

*Approximately two million French prisoners of war were incarcerated in Germany. Most had been arrested before the armistice, June 22, 1940.

In December, in the middle of the afternoon, my parents' doorbell rang. I went to open it. It was a police officer.

"We're looking for Monsieur Brull."

I panicked. In the dark, behind him, was the grey-green uniform of a German soldier.

"He's not here."

The policeman didn't move, accustomed no doubt to this miserable attempt at deception.

"No point in lying, we know he's here. We were waiting in the concierge's loge and we saw him pass by."

My throat went dry. That bitch of a concierge . . .

Smelling of cold air and cheap tobacco, he pushed past me without asking and entered the living room, as if he were at home. There was my mother, ashen, and my father, standing proud and straight. He had seen death up close during the war. No ordinary policeman would make him go to pieces.

"Monsieur Brull?"

He gave the briefest of nods.

"Get your things. You're coming with us."

He made no attempt to explain and produced no paperwork. His voice was without affect, neither kind nor mean. It was simply an order that could not be disputed.

A deadly silence fell on the apartment. Maurice appeared, then Bijou, her eyes wide in disbelief. She hid against my mother's hip when she saw the German soldier. I heard my father moving about in his room; he came back with a small suitcase, as if he were going off for a few days, and then calmly kissed us all.

"I'll be back soon, children."

His manner was cool and calm, without so much as a glance toward his two guards.

Quietly, he held my mother and kissed her.

"You know my friends at the Ministry," he added. "You know whom to go see."

Then he disappeared from the apartment, followed by the German soldier. The three sets of footsteps echoed for a long time in the bottomless silence that followed.

Maurice was sixteen. Papa never saw him again.

That was a blow we never saw coming.

Why my father? Had he been involved in activities we knew nothing about?

The police were arresting people, everyone knew that. But for now they were only arresting foreign Jews, like the ones I sometimes saw at the hospital when they were sick. There were roundups all the time, completely random, in restaurants, in the métro, at police check points. But in theory, French Jews were not being picked up. So why my father? Especially since his status as hero of the Great War and employee at the Ministry was supposed to protect him. Why?

The following day, there was no news. Nor the day after that.

My mother laid siege to police headquarters and sought help from friends of my father at the Ministry.

"His name is Samuel Brull. A French police officer came for him. With a German soldier."

"Oh! With a German. Then you need to go see the German authorities."

"I went to see them yesterday, but they wouldn't speak to me. There was a French police officer. . . . So someone *here* has to know where they've taken him."

"Do you know the name of the officer? What section he's in?"

"No, he said nothing. He didn't even show us any papers."

"Then I can't help you. You need to ask the Germans."

My mother remained calm. She explained that she had just come back from there, from the *kommandatur*, and that she would return there as much as she had to, but for right now, she was here, at French police headquarters. And that her husband had been arrested by a French policeman, *also*. The official's face crumpled.

"Disappearances and arrests, they happen every day. . . . Were his papers in order, at least? You've registered as Jews?"

"Yes, they were in order. We all have our papers in order. I can show you mine. He works for the Ministry."

"I know, you've already told me that. And at the Ministry, you've inquired? Maybe they know something . . ."

In general, no one wanted to get dragged into this. If a German had arrested him, this Brull, it was because something was not right. It might be too dangerous to get involved. Some people were openly happy about what was going on. Too bad for the Yids, they had it coming.

■ January 1942.
At home, at the hospital or at school, the days dragged on, endless. What could they have done with him? If he had been interned in Drancy or one of the camps in the Loiret, we should have found out about it. Why this silence?

Finally, it must have been the second or third of January, my mother came home with some news. Our father was neither missing nor dead but interned at a camp in Compiègne. As a hostage.

Now here was a roundup of a different order. Jacques told me that this was the first time French Jews had been arrested, those whom Pétain was supposed to protect.

"They arrested more than seven hundred people, but not just anybody, you'll be proud to hear, Colette," he said, ironically. "The upper

crust, only the most prominent. It seems they have Léon Blum's brother*
and Tristan Bernard's son.** They put them in a makeshift prison in an
indoor riding arena at the military school. Now they are all at Royallieu, a camp near Compiègne. It's an old barracks, and it seems to be
run directly by the Nazis."

I shuddered. Why were they hostages?

Along with my father, the others were older men in important posi-
tions: the most well-respected lawyers, men from liberal professions.
Stupid, gloating articles appeared in the anti-Semitic press. *At last,
France is being purged!* These headlines made me sick. I wanted to take
the papers, tear them up and stomp on them. My father had fought for
France, he managed factories, and now he was at the Ministry. Purge
France? Of what?

A major exhibition had just opened: *Le Juif et la France.* Huge pan-
els showed the public what Jews looked like, why Jews were dangerous,
parasites to be rooted out of society, from every aspect of society. So now
that the purge was indeed happening, people should be pleased. But
Jacques told me that the exhibition was not as successful as anticipated
and that made me happy.

My mother was not able to get approval to write to my father. We
simply learned some time later that he had been transferred to Drancy.

"He has a right to one parcel a week. We can put in some clean clothes
and things to eat, but only canned goods and cookies. Anything else

---

*René Blum, the younger brother of the prime minister of France, Léon Blum, was him-
self a beloved and respected figure. He founded the Ballets Russes of Monte-Carlo. Arrested by the Germans in December 1941, he was sent to the German-run concentration
camp, Royallieu-Compiègne, then deported. He died in Auschwitz.

**Jean-Jacques Bernard, playwright and son of popular playwright Tristan Bernard, was
arrested along with 743 eminent French Jewish citizens and sent to Royallieu-Compiègne.
Bernard was released in March 1942. His memoir, *The Camp of Slow Death*, is a devastating
account of this experience.

will be confiscated. And not more than two kilos," she told us, sounding a bit relieved.

We learned very soon that the camp guards shamelessly looted most of the parcels before the prisoners ever got them.

"And Papa, can we go see him?" She shook her head, expressionless.

"No, no visits. And I've had no success finding out how long he'll be there. But your father has connections. He is after all a lieutenant colonel in the reserves and a war hero. I am sure we can get him released."

We had the right to write him letters, but no more than fifteen lines, and letters were opened. Any infraction of these rules would be severely punished.

A few days later we received another visit, from an employee at the Ministry where Papa worked.

"This is for you," he said, handing my mother an envelope. "It's your husband's salary for the month of January."

She turned pale.

"He won't be paid anymore?"

"No, I am sorry. . . ."

Shamefaced, the accountant left quickly.

We all looked at Maman. The bank accounts of Jews had been blocked. For the four of us to live, we now had only my tiny pay as an intern at the Rothschild Hospital, an amount that lasted only three or four days for me.

But certainly not for four people, and two of them growing children.

My mother took a deep breath. She had always lived in affluence with no material worries, and yet faced with this new situation, she did not panic. After all, she had left the comforts of Tunisia to rejoin her husband—in the middle of a war, yet. The hardships were material ones. And we would resolve them materially.

Overnight her expression had changed.

She had a new look about her, stronger and more resolute. Maybe it was her father's look, Moïse who had arrived in Tunisia as poor as Job and made a fortune by the sweat of his brow. And this told me many things—*We are going to fight. I am going to get your father out of there, and you, you are going to help me. War or no war.*

8

The Star

■ My mother now consulted me for important decisions. With that concierge collaborating with the Germans, our apartment in the fourteenth arrondissement had become too dangerous. We had to get out as soon as possible. She explained to me that Papa had anticipated our flight some time ago. He had rented an apartment on avenue Hoche, not far from where he had been working. But his surprise internment had stymied our move.

He had even foreseen the need for some backup inside the building. This was Monsieur Drogue, a veteran, a retired noncommissioned officer, with whom he got along very well. We explained our situation to him and he immediately agreed to help us. The operation was planned in two stages. One evening, very late, we moved as much furniture as we could into two servants' rooms on the top floor. The next morning, taking advantage of the concierge's absence—she had gone out in search of provisions—we sneaked out with our luggage, leaving no forwarding address. The old bag would no longer be sticking her nose into our business. And she would not know where we were living.

Monsieur Drogue promised to get our mail to us and, most importantly, inform us if the police started to make inquiries about us.

The move did not change our daily routine. I continued to attend classes at the school on rue Cuvier, and every day I went to Rothschild, where I grew more and more fond of the group we formed around

Mademoiselle Damangout, Gougoutte. The majority were interns like myself. Something was drawing us together; we felt perhaps the same rebelliousness, the same desire to do something. Without anything being said aloud, of course.

I regularly ran into a young woman, about thirty years old— Claire Heyman, who was Jewish, unmarried, and had worked at Rothschild for several years. She was the social worker for the hospital and while very close to Gougoutte, she didn't mingle with our little circle, which made the pharmacy lab our general headquarters. Claire Heyman was tall and slim with long, light brown hair, always elegant, even-tempered, ever smiling, but very reserved. Just looking at her, it would be hard to suspect any irregularity in her conduct, and I certainly would have been very surprised if I'd been told she was preparing to be the brains behind an escape network, a leader of clandestine warfare.

We didn't know then that for her this war against the Nazis had commenced some years before, since Kristallnacht, November 1938, that monstrous pogrom triggered by the Nazis after the assassination of a German diplomat in Paris. A number of Jewish organizations had at that time taken on the rescue and relocation of orphans to France. Claire Heyman had played a part in this.* I imagine that her heart must have been breaking as she witnessed the fate reserved for foreign Jews, this time in France. When they were arrested, some of them had to abandon their children, and somebody had to care for them. So Claire was already on the front lines, ready to act and train us for action.

Particularly since the noose was tightening.

*After Kristallnacht, Baroness Germaine de Rothschild organized a Kindertransport operation from Germany, rescuing 130 Jewish children who then received care at the Rothschild Hospital under Claire Heyman's supervision.

In the spring, the French authorities readied a new humiliation for us, this time even worse. The news raced through the hospital like wildfire. We couldn't believe it. Would this really never stop?

My mother was waiting for me at home, her face stiff, as if she felt personally insulted.

"I guess you know," she said.

"Yes, I heard."

Just talking about it, I had tears in my voice, a knot in my stomach.

"We don't have a choice, Colette. I'm going to the town hall to find out where to get them, these stars. You'll help me sew them on, they have to be on all our clothes."

A few days later we had a sewing bee, in silence. I sewed around the edges of a patch of yellow fabric bearing a star of David outlined in black. In the center, in large, vaguely Gothic letters was written the word JUIF.

I who had never liked sewing . . .

The rules were very strict: the star had to be firmly sewn on and clearly visible on the left side of the chest. It was forbidden to try to hide it. Absolutely forbidden not to wear it, under pain of arrest or deportation. This time we were truly cornered.

Bijou watched me, curious. "It's for children, too?"

"From the age of six, yes."

"And at school, too?"

"At school, too. But since you don't go to school . . ."

Since our move, we made the decision not to send my little sister to school, even though she was nine years old. Instinctively, Maman had understood that we had better be as invisible as possible. Maurice continued to attend the lycée. He stared at me while Maman was sewing on his star. He was pale, silent, his jaw clenched.

The next day, I walked very slowly, sensing everyone's eyes upon me. I arrived at the métro station, my cheeks burning, my face impassive. This first foray outside was horrific, and this time I had no choice: I was marked as a Jew and Jews were allowed in the rear carriage only. I collapsed onto the seat, feeling as if I'd run a marathon. There were five or six of us with our yellow stars, staring stonily at each other. An old woman, a man who looked like an office worker, a mother and her son with light eyes and freckled cheeks. The métro started up, and my eyes lost focus in the noisy darkness of the tunnel.

Shame and rage struggled within me, but my cries died in my throat. What good were they?

Not all French people approved. At times I noticed glances that were pained, ashamed. This was not right. This was not France. Others looked us up and down with condescension, with nasty satisfaction—I looked daggers at them.

One day, an elderly gentleman entered the Jews' carriage. He was old, very distinguished, impeccably dressed, wearing his military medals. A member of the upper class, very *vieille France*. He was not wearing the yellow star.

"Ah!" he exclaimed, loudly. "At last, a clean spot. It's the only place on this train where one can feel comfortable!"

And then he sat down, maintaining his dignity. I was touched and felt tears of gratitude.

At the Faculté de Médecine, two classmates, the Bourguignon brothers, came looking for me in these very first days of the star.

"Colette," the older one said to me, "you must find stars for us as well. We'll wear them with you."

I was surprised and vigorously refused.

"No way! There are people who've done that and they've had problems."

These were stories circulating here and there, no one knew if they were true. As a sign of protest, some young Aryans—non-Jews in the ridiculous Nazi idiom—had sported yellow stars with various inscriptions: *Catholic*, *Protestant*, *Zazou*, or even *Papou* or *Swing*. It seems they were arrested—not surprising, because the Nazis had absolutely no sense of humor.

However, the Bourguignon brothers insisted. "Too bad, we don't care. We want a star!"

"No. Absolutely not!"

"OK, OK. But in that case, we're going to accompany you everywhere."

And from that day, the Bourguignon brothers were my two bodyguards at school. I never had any problems there.

Just after this new *decoration* was rolled out, I had to take the exams at the end of my second year. I had worked hard, and I was trembling when I entered the huge oak-paneled amphitheater. Seated there were three examiners—a jury president and two others. I needed an average grade to pass. One of them called me:

"Mademoiselle Brull!"

I went forward and stood in front of him.

He asked me a rather simple question in bacteriology but didn't give me time to even open my mouth.

"You know nothing. I'm giving you a zero."

His face betrayed a malicious satisfaction. Clearly he was enjoying the situation. What a pleasure to humiliate a little Jewish student! I gasped with surprise. He took advantage of this to dismiss me, cutting me off again.

I could still do a makeup interview with the jury president. So I sat down on a bench in the corridor, my throat dry, and waited for the exams to end. If they were all like the first examiner, I could kiss my medical studies goodbye.

His face unreadable, the president bade me enter. He, too, examined my star, my records. He sighed. At that moment I was sure he was about to give me the final blow.

"So it seems you got a zero," he said. "You didn't know anything?" I straightened up, still bursting with anger.

"No, that's not it at all. The examiner prevented me from answering and gave me a zero."

The president sighed again and looked once more at the star on my chest. He thought for a few moments before speaking. Maybe he was looking for some other, more subtle way to drive the dagger even deeper. But not at all:

"Can you tell me what question he asked you?"

I told him what the topic had been. He sighed once more and then allowed me to speak. This time without interruption. At the end of this session, he gave me a nine out of ten—a mark that was certainly inflated—and delivered it with a smile.

"You've passed your second year, Mademoiselle."

So we Jews were not totally alone.

▨ "Colette, I have to talk to you," Jacques said to me.

He had been looking a bit glum for a few days now, but that hadn't worried me too much.

Who could feel happy in our circumstances? After work, we retreated to a bistro near the hospital.

"I will not wear the star."

"Yes, I already noticed you're not wearing it. But you'd better be careful. If you are arrested, they could send you to Drancy."

"That's not what I meant. I won't wear the star because I'm leaving for the Free Zone.* Could you . . . do you think you could . . . would you like to come with me?"

I wasn't expecting that; my heart beat faster. He could not have found a clearer way to tell me that I mattered to him, that he could no longer think of his own life without thinking of mine.

"No, Jacques, it's out of the question. My father is in Drancy. Maman is alone with my brother and sister. I can't leave them. Do you understand that?"

"I thought so," he answered simply. "But I am not staying. There is nothing more for us to do here."

He was referring obviously to the hospital, which was looking more and more like a prison. Maybe he was right, that we should flee. Maybe if I had been alone, I would have gone with him, for I already knew I was going to miss him.

"My older sister is already in the Free Zone. I'm going to join her with my mother."

"You know how you are going to manage it?"

The Jews had begun to flee Paris en masse. The star was a serious threat, they now had files on us, and foreign Jews were interned. Those who could afford it took the train south, looking everywhere for ways to cross the line of demarcation. The wealthiest or the smartest got themselves false papers. But many were like Jacques, who just took off trusting to luck, with fear in their bellies.

"There are all kinds of ways to cross the line," he said. "I've got a little money, I'll find a way."

---

*The Free Zone (Vichy, also called Unoccupied Zone) was that part of France not yet occupied by the Germans and separated from the North by the line of demarcation.

Our eyes met again. I tried to breathe normally. I wouldn't let myself cry in front of him.

"One day, everything will turn out all right," he said to me. "And we will write to each other."

I'd already seen those postcards, the only mail authorized between the Occupied Zone and the Unoccupied Zone. The words were already filled in, you just crossed out the irrelevant ones:

- *in good health*
- *tired*
- *slightly, seriously ill, wounded*
- *killed*
- *prisoner*
- *deceased*
- *no news*

And so on for a dozen or more lines.

You could send *warm thoughts* or *kisses*, write in two additional lines by hand and sign it. Any card with wording not strictly related to family matters would be destroyed. Some of my friends said that if you worked out coded words in advance, you could manage to say a bit more. Poor ploys that didn't get you far.

Heartbroken, we said goodbye. He turned to give me a final wave, he may have been smiling but already I could no longer see his face. He then disappeared into the shadows for good.

We exchanged two or three of these interzone cards and then I had no more news.

Stars were in full bloom at the hospital, a bizarre epidemic of yellow cloth on our immaculate coats. White coats, yellow stars. Some wore stars made of celluloid to respect the rules of hygiene.

Something in our eyes had changed, but it was not only there. Our sick or surgical patients from various camps described very harsh conditions. Most of these prisons had been set up in haste, like Drancy, where the detainees first slept on the concrete floors, without heat or hygiene, and little food. In the first weeks, about thirty of them died of exhaustion or sickness. It had since improved a bit, they told us, but they all continued to suffer from hunger, cold, and all kinds of shortages. There were twenty faucets for several thousand detainees, dysentery, vermin, lice, bedbugs, and the despair of not knowing what the future held. The Red Cross was able to establish an office there and that is where we took parcels for our father.

Besides the star, two events caused us to start thinking differently. First, attacks against the occupier had multiplied since the invasion of the USSR and were systematically followed by the execution of French hostages. The latter were often seized from among the Jews interned at Drancy or elsewhere. Every prisoner therefore lived in permanent danger of being shot.

The other thing that made us very anxious was the departure of Jews by train: in March 1942, the first convoy left the camp at Royallieu, where my father had first been interned. No one knew where it was headed. The *déportés*, it was thought, must be going to some type of forced labor camp in a settlement colony somewhere. Kibbutzes, in short, but not exactly the kind we used to dream of. At first I thought these camps must be in Normandy or some other part of France, but that was just nonsense. The trains, in fact, were going to the East. To Germany? Or farther, to Poland?

No one knew.

As a consequence, our priorities at the hospital made an about-face. Now we did whatever we could to keep the detainees as long as possible. It was the best way to prevent their return to Drancy and possible deportation. There was no open call or order to that effect, but it was obvious to me and my small group of friends. Later, I understood that it had all come from Claire Heyman. From the very first train departures, she must have figured it out, devised solutions, and no doubt reactivated her contacts.

Very quickly, however, we realized that not everyone wanted to play this game.

Doctor H., head of surgery, was scared stiff. Sick internees in his department, once they were well enough, were returned to Drancy immediately. There was no question of them staying a minute longer.

One day, the police picked up a poor Jewish fellow on the streets; he had no papers and was half dead from hunger and devoured by lice. We treated him, scrubbed him clean, and put him back on his feet as quick as a wink. And it turned out that the cops at the main entrance were on our side. Send him to Drancy? There was no hurry. . . .

"Keep him a bit longer, things will settle down. No one's come looking for him, you understand? . . ."

Unambiguous collusion. *Keep him inside where it's warm, the poor fellow. With a little luck, maybe we can get him out in a few days.* So even among the police, not everyone agreed with these internments and deportations.

But H. didn't see it that way. Once he heard about this, he got on his high horse: "Oh no, I don't want trouble! He's been looked after and now he gets handed back to the police."

The poor man was taken to the police station and most likely interned in a camp. This story spread quickly through the whole hospital.

With H. as head of surgery, an appendicitis stay was five days, although it really could have been at least eight. It was the same for every other operation. Moreover, any interns who tried to persuade him to prolong hospitalizations were dismissed.

"I don't want trouble," was H.'s systematic reply. "It's no."

"But he's in no condition to . . ."

He neither examined the patient nor looked at his file. He didn't want trouble, period, and that was that.

"In no condition to, in no condition to, what does that mean? Does he have a fever? Are there complications?"

"No, but look, he's weak. . . ."

"I already told you no. I don't want trouble in my department. He's been operated on. What more do you want?"

"His incision hasn't healed yet. . . ."

H. would stiffen, his features taut with anger and fear.

"Of course, it hasn't healed yet. It will later and he'll get his dressings and care at Drancy, like the others. Five days is five days! He's on the list to go, so that's it! He's going!"

He would turn his back and the conversation would end there.

We had to find ways around this. The young interns in surgery often came to see us in despair, and we helped out as much as we could.

"He's just had an operation on the pelvis. He's supposed to leave in two days."

"How is he doing?"

The intern pulled a face.

"OK. It went all right. He's a strong guy. I told him not to look too healthy, but you know H. . . . . . All the same, I'm going to tell him there's a complication."

Everything was backward: now we worried when a convalescence went too well, when incisions healed too quickly. That was bad news for the patient. We had to get him away from H. as quickly as possible.

"A complication, absolutely not," I said. "H. will get anxious and want to stick his nose in. I'd rather tell him there's a risk of pneumonia.

In that way, he'll get out of the surgery pavilion. I'll go talk it over with Gougoutte. You go talk to Leibovici. He'll find that pneumonia for us all right."

Marcel Leibovici was a Romanian doctor, one of the interns most experienced in surgery. A guy I had confidence in, someone who like us tried to prolong patients' stays.

We took a quick look around. It was life as usual: nurses walking between pavilions, their arms full of vials and flasks, and visitors, some of them wearing the yellow star.

A few of us made up these ruses—albeit without the slightest knowledge of what happened when the trains arrived at Birkenau or elsewhere. A case of pneumonia meant a few days of respite, or perhaps enough time for these prisoners to contact family members who were still at liberty and ask them for help in trying to get released.

At the time we really resented H. After all, he was Jewish like us, trapped, confronted with the same harassment, the same problems we all had. At the end of the war some people lashed out at him. He had been *despicable*, never had he tried to help those who resisted, not even a little. He had to be punished.

But I never gave evidence against him. Punish him for what? For having been afraid? How many people were guilty of that?

Fortunately, not everyone behaved like he did. Even though they were closely surveilled by the Nazis or their henchmen, other head doctors became our allies, quietly turning a blind eye when certain patients stayed on longer for no particular reason. For instance, there was Isch-Wall, my superior, or Paul Walther, the head of maternity, Gaston Nora, or Robert Worms.

Of course, I thought about Papa. At Drancy he was in constant danger of being deported or shot as a hostage. The uncertainty was horrible and sometimes woke me at night.

Maman and I talked at length about him. What if we tried to get him hospitalized at Rothschild? Once there, maybe we could make use of our contacts, get him freed for health reasons.

This plan had one drawback—Papa was in hopelessly good health. At least so we believed.

■ Within a few weeks, a solid bond united us, like comrades in arms. There were some people who looked away and did nothing, and some who were afraid. Those were the people we could not trust, and in front of whom we said nothing. And then there were others, those who acted and took risks. We did not talk to each other, we didn't know what the others were doing; everything took place through words dropped here and there, a look or a gesture.

There were five or six of us who formed a group around Gougoutte. I became close to Simon Schwartz, a pharmacy intern with a mop of brown hair and horn-rimmed glasses that made him look like Harold Lloyd. His father had disappeared, which plunged his family into terrible difficulties, like my own. They had nothing to eat. I also got to be good friends with Lison, a lab assistant my age, and with another intern named Spiegelman. Only one doctor was admitted to our clique, Hirsch-Marie, the doctor in charge of the laboratory.

We often met in the duty room for what the administration called lunch. Of all the hospitals in Paris, Rothschild was ranked lowest—and the most poorly served. This could be seen in the meals. Meat appeared only once a week and it was always disgusting.

Often it was *beef lung*, a small piece of esophagus with attached alveoli floating in a watery sauce.

Our stomachs would revolt and we would regale each other with thoughts of *real chocolate, real butter,* or *real bread*, the food of kings, the taste of which now seemed lost to us forever. And in an attempt to forget these tastes, we all started to cook in our own fashion. Despite the almost complete lack of every ingredient, I turned out to be quite a decent cook.

My masterpiece was a *pâté sans viande*, a pâté without meat, a clever recipe made from kneaded yeast and boiled onions.

"Ah, Colette's pâté without meat!" exclaimed my friends when I brought them my delicious treat.

And with a glimmer of delight in our eyes, we savored my strange meatless meatballs, a weird recipe I have never dared to reproduce since.

I think back to the laboratory, which had become our headquarters, with its empty flasks and white tiles. Aside from Gougoutte and Dr. Hirsch-Marie, we were all in our early twenties, and we felt confident enough in our select group to talk about the war. At that moment, events were completely depressing—the Nazis were winning everywhere. True, they had not succeeded in landing in England or taking Moscow, but their armies occupied all of Europe and a part of Africa, where they had just seized Tobruk. Their Japanese allies had destroyed the American fleet at Pearl Harbor, a disaster that left the taste of ashes. If the Americans were wiped out even before getting into the game, it truly was the end of everything.

"They are going to invade Australia," some people said.

"It hasn't happened yet. The boches keep saying they're going to take Moscow and Leningrad, but we're still waiting on that one. And we haven't heard the last from Father Stalin."

"Yeah. Well, yeah, it's about time we start hearing from him, your Stalin."

Though it was forbidden by the authorities, we all listened to Radio London.

"Did you hear? It seems that the French Forces under de Gaulle have beaten the Germans in Libya."

"We heard, no need to shout."

"At Bir Hakeim."

"They weren't beaten, the boches, they were just delayed. I thought I understood that they got through all the same and that Rommel would soon be in Cairo."

"He's not there yet. We'll see."

We never let our guard down while we were talking, and regularly kept an eye on the corridor.

The discussions went on for hours, under the benevolent eye of Gougoutte. The most astonishing thing was that each of us ended up playing our part in the underground network that helped children escape, Mademoiselle Damangout being the first and foremost.

But never for one moment did we talk about it. Neither during the war nor after it.

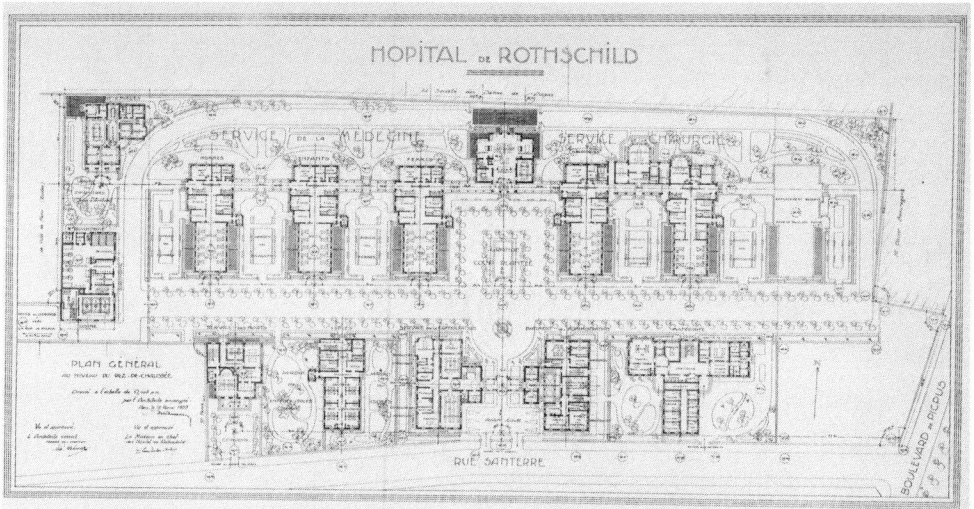

Figure 1

Architectural drawing of the Rothschild Hospital. The hospital was inaugurated in 1914 on land newly purchased on the rue Santerre, replacing a smaller hospital on the rue de Picpus. The drawing depicts a series of pavilions in a parklike setting. The building at lower left was the morgue with its own entrance, which Colette Brull-Ulmann and others used to smuggle children from the hospital to safe-houses. (AN/IFA. Paris. Fonds Bechmann. Cote IFA 47/17)

Figure 2

View of the Rothschild Hospital from rue de Picpus, 1914. The building on the left is the maternity pavilion, where mothers were asked to give up their newborns to be smuggled to safety. To the right is the Picpus Cemetery, site of a skirmish between Resistance and the French Militia during the insurrection of Paris. The cemetery is the burial site of the Marquis de La Fayette. (AN/IFA. Paris. Fonds Bechmann. Cote IFA 47/17)

Figure 3
The Rothschild Hospital main entrance and adjoining administrative pavilion have been preserved as a site of memory. In 1954, the Rothschild family donated the hospital to the public hospital system of Paris (AP-HP) for one symbolic franc. The other buildings have since been modified or demolished, and Rothschild is now a modern facility. (Landau Collection)

Figure 4
Main entrance. To the left was the police checkpoint; to the right, the receptionists' office. The receptionists alerted staff when Gestapo or French police wagons approached the gate. In 1944, two receptionists were arrested and deported. (Landau Collection)

Figure 5
One of many plaques in the Rothschild Hospital administrative pavilion
memorializing hospital and medical personnel who were deported and murdered.
(Landau Collection)

Figure 6
Claire Heyman was the Rothschild Hospital social worker to whom
Colette Brull-Ulmann dedicated her memoir. Responsible for the
hospital's clandestine network, Heyman procured false death certificates
and baptism certificates and found hideouts for children in convents and
with child rescue organizations. As she never spoke about her activities,
the scope of her organization remains a mystery. (Pierronet Collection)

37759

Délégation F.F.C.I.

...serne de la Pépinière **ATTESTATION**

Rue Laborde

d'appartenance aux F.F.C.

Aucun duplicata ne pouvant être délivré, le porteur de la présente attestation ne devra s'en dessaisir en aucune circonstance et, en cas de besoin, faire établir des copies conformes —

Original à conserver

par l'intéressé **RÉFÉRENCES**

D. M. N° 2843/CAB/MIL du 24-1-45.
D. M. N° 4842/EMA/1 du 11-4-45.
D. M. N° 7907/EMA/1 du 31-4-45.
D. M. N° 8863/EMA/1 du 21-6-45.

Fiche n° 11.082/EMA/1 du 3-8-45.
Feuille de renseignements
n° 11.529/EMA/1 du 10-8-45.
I. M. N. 13.172/EMA/1 du 12-9-45.
I. M. N. 17-216/RS/R/1 du 6-11-45.

11e
Monsieur _____ BRULL Colette _____, né le 18.4.1920

a signé un contract d'engagement en application du décret 366 da 25 juillet 1942.

Réseau : _____ GOELETTE

Arrêté le _____ -- _____ Rapatrié le _____ --

Les services accomplis **comme agent P 2** comptent

du ___ 1.4.1944 ___ au ___ 30.9.1944

en qualité de _____ Chargé _____ de mission de _5éme_ classe,

Grade correspondant homologué par la Commission nationale d'homologation : _Sergent Chef_ (pendant la durée de la mission).

Paris, le _____ 20 Mars _____ 1948

CERTIFIÉ EXACT :

Le Lt. Colonel LE CARS
chef du bureau liquidateur des **Forces Françaises
Combattantes de l'Intérieur**

Les services accomplis en qualité d'Agent P2 conformément au dispositions du 366 du 15-7-1942 comptent comme **services militaires actifs.**

J. Z. 832055

Figure 7
Official document attesting that Colette Brull-Ulmann belonged to the Goelette resistance network, part of the FFC (French Fighting Forces). Her rank was staff sergeant. (Brull-Ulmann Collection)

Figure 8
False identity papers were common during the German Occupation.
Underground, Colette Brull became Colette Mosnier as she moved about Paris,
smuggling children and collecting intelligence. (Brull-Ulmann Collection)

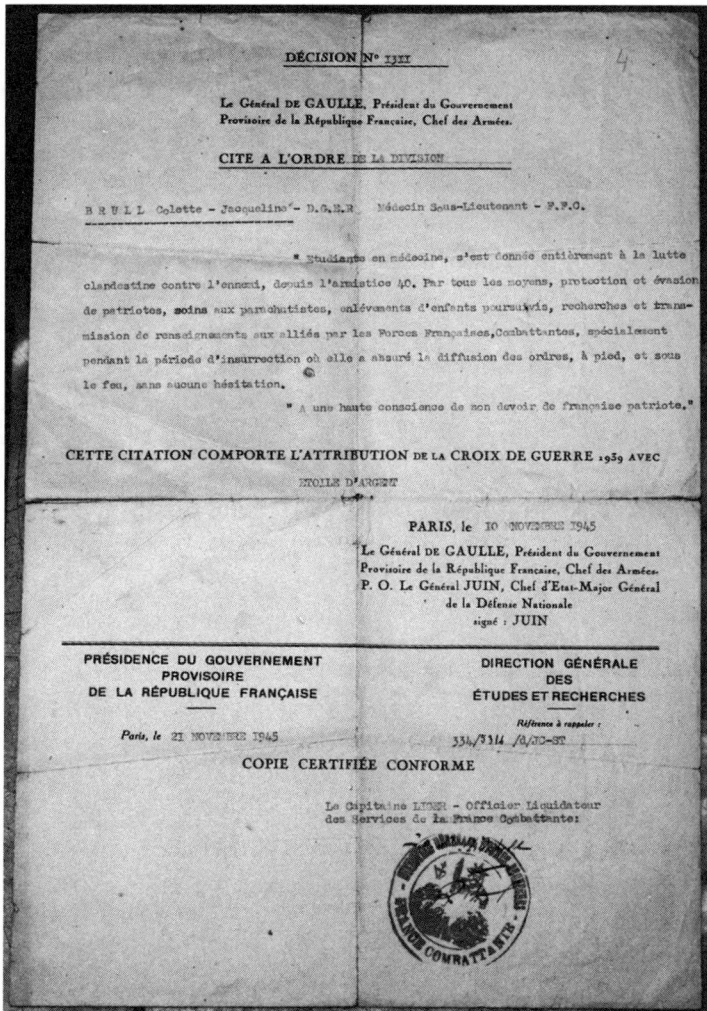

Figure 9

General de Gaulle awarded Colette Brull-Ulmann the Croix de Guerre with Silver Star for "protecting and aiding patriots to escape, providing care to parachutists, rescuing hunted children, seeking and transmitting intelligence to the Allies through the French Fighting Forces, especially during the insurrection when she delivered orders, on foot, and under fire, without hesitation." She demonstrated a "keen understanding of her duty as a patriotic Frenchwoman." (Brull-Ulmann Collection)

Figure 10

"The American people would like to express its gratitude for your contribution to the allied cause during enemy occupation. Your aid to our fighters fallen in France merits the esteem and recognition of the Government of the United States." (Brull-Ulmann Collection)

9
Hard Times

Since Papa's imprisonment our situation had become very hard. Not only did we have no regular income (apart from my minuscule intern's pay), but worse, the German laws against the Jews were unrelenting.

It was forbidden to own a radio or bicycle. *Verboten* to have a telephone at one's home or to use public phone booths, to go to museums, swimming pools, restaurants, public gardens. We no longer had the right to change residence.

Obligatory curfew from eight in the evening to six in the morning.

One evening two policemen came to seize the only bicycle we had, which belonged to Maurice. I opened the door and they told me peremptorily why they had come. I drew myself up to my full height and shot back:

"Sorry, someone already *swiped* it before you."

As they stared me down, taken aback, I explained that my brother had been robbed of his bike a month earlier, in front of the house.

"You can check on it. We reported it to your police station."

They turned to leave, their shoulders slumped.

But that wasn't the worst of it.

One day in July, I was indignant to learn that we no longer could do our shopping at the same hours as everyone else. We were restricted to one hour, between three and four in the afternoon.

This news seemed so unbelievably cruel that it took me an entire day to be convinced it was true. Yet this was really what the government had imposed on us. There was no end to the baseness, the cruelty. It was pretty much condemning us to starve to death. My mother, normally so proud, was not able to hide her distress.

"Do you realize what this means? People are already in line at eight in the morning. By midday there is nothing left in the stores. What do you expect me to find at three o'clock!"

And of course it was impossible to get around it. The word JUIF appeared in big letters on our ration coupons.

I tried to reassure Maman, who was wringing her hands. "There's the black market, right?"

"But what can we pay with, Colette? With your pay? That only lasts for two days."

"We need to dig into our savings. Papa had some savings, didn't he?"

She shook her head. "We can't touch them. All bank accounts have been blocked."

"What then? What are we going to do?"

It was my turn to feel the blow. Now we really had a knife at our throats. I thought about Maurice and Bijou, their malnourished faces, their disappointment when Maman put food on their plates each night. What would we give them to eat? Should we flee Paris? But where would we go? And with what money? And that would also mean abandoning Papa, that we no longer believed he'd be released, that perhaps he, too, would leave on their train.

I was so stunned that I barely noticed my mother's hand on my arm.

"Don't look so glum. Maybe there's a solution."

I saw her pointing at the rest of the apartment, which was bathed in shadow.

"We have things we can sell. Some of the furniture is worth a little money and your father has his collection of bronzes. It's only that . . . it's forbidden for us to go to the public pawn shop, the *mont-de-piété*.* We'll have to find another way."

A friend of my father, a Monsieur Beau, bought—at a fair price—a small seventeenth-century painting belonging to my parents, and a Louis XIV sideboard, both very valuable.

He paid for everything in cash, but this bonanza lasted only a few weeks. From then on, every week or two, Maman gave me silver cutlery, chandeliers, platters, or porcelain, anything at all valuable, and I'd set off on the hunt. The moment they saw me push open the doors, with my star on my chest, the shopkeepers knew why I had come. I was not the only one doing this in Paris. Most of the time, I was taken to the back to display my small wares.

Sometimes, the examination was superficial and took only a few seconds. At other times, the shopkeeper at least took the trouble to examine the hallmark through his magnifying glass.

"I'll give you fifty francs."

"Fifty francs? But it's silverware. And almost brand new!"

"That's all I can offer you. And I'm being kind. At that price, I'm still doing you a favor."

On average, my buyers proposed prices ten or fifteen times less than the true value. And there was no way to argue about it. I was too proud to beg, to explain that without this money two children were going to starve to death. And I also guessed it wouldn't have made much of a difference to them.

*Mont-de-Piété de Paris (Crédit Municipal de Paris). A national pawnshop owned and operated by the city of Paris since 1777, where items are deposited in exchange for a cash loan. If the depositor is unable to reimburse the loan after an agreed-upon period of time, the asset is sold at auction.

In any case, my attempts at negotiations always ended the same way.

"So? Have you made up your mind? I haven't got all day, Mademoiselle."

I'd go out the door, drained, and sickened with shame and anger. People who had nothing, what did they do? Sometimes in the métro I'd see Jews, their clothes threadbare, their eyes feverish, exhausted, and terrified, like animals caught in a trap.

And I'd tell myself that we would end up looking like them.

So while I made the rounds of antique dealers and secondhand shops in between my classes and my shifts at Rothschild, my mother continued to move heaven and earth in an effort to get my father released from Drancy. Without him, we couldn't hold on much longer.

She tried to get an influential lawyer to intervene, a member of UGIF (General Union of the Jews of France).* No luck. She often talked about one of my father's former students, Georges Lamirand, who was now Minister for Youth in the Pétain government.**

"Our families have remained very close," she tried to persuade herself. "Do you remember that you and Yoyo were bridesmaids at his wedding?"

"Of course I remember. But you haven't heard a peep out of him."

---

*UGIF. The Union Générale des Israélites de France was a body set up in November 1941 to represent the Jews of France with the public authorities. It was controlled by the Commissariat général aux questions juives (General Commissariat for Jewish Affairs), and its role was controversial. It has been reproached for leaving to the mercy of the Nazis children and orphans in its charge who could have been hidden.

**Georges Lamirand (1899–1994) was secretary general in charge of Youth Affairs in the Vichy government from September 1940 to March 1943. At his trial in 1947, his case was dismissed. He had protected Jews and tried to convince Pétain to go to North Africa when the Germans invaded the Unoccupied Zone in November 1942. He later served many years as mayor of La Bourboule.

"He's a good man who likes your father a lot. He promised to help us. I'm sure he'll come through."

But Lamirand did not seem to have much sway. Worse . . . we learned that *Le Pilori*, the anti-Semitic rag of the time, had its sights on him. Their reporters claimed that Lamirand was sleeping with the wife and daughter of a Yid whose affairs he was interested in. They didn't name names, but it was obviously us. It seemed that Papa had powerful enemies.

So we decided to go for broke.

Since my father was at Drancy, we were allowed to write him—fifteen lines, no more, systematically read by the guards. But from his very first letter, he found a way around this.

This is what he wrote:

I want Colette to get me some eye drops that I absolutely must have for my eyes. They will be good for what I've got. Here's the formula . . .

What came next was a chemical compound that in no way corresponded to any medication. And besides, my father didn't wear glasses.

"I don't understand," worried my mother. "He's got something wrong with his eyes now?"

"This isn't medicine. I'll find out what it is at the lab tomorrow."

The next day the lab confirmed that this was definitely not a medical product. It took me a few days to understand:

Must have for my eyes . . . Good for what I've got.

It was a formula for invisible ink! I had it made up, and it was a clear, odorless liquid. I wrote a few lines with a pen. The words were invisible, but when the paper was heated, they appeared in blue. After several not very successful tries on white paper, which showed traces of the ink, I was able to get quite a good result on brown wrapping paper.

Thanks to these unique eye drops, we were able to correspond with my father. The letter that was authorized, the one they opened, was filled with banalities. The real message was written in invisible ink on the package wrapping. Very quickly, the question of escape arose.

Papa knew the situation we were in. He knew we couldn't hold on much longer without him; he needed to get back to us.

The public housing buildings at Drancy, in the shape of a *U*, were surrounded by barbed wire and flanked with watchtowers at each of the four corners. My father, a veteran of the trenches, was quick to see a weakness: a blind spot where the wire would be relatively easy to cut provided you had wire cutters, which obviously were not available in the camp.

I was put in charge of procuring one. On the advice of my father, I asked Monsieur Drogue, our old neighbor in the fourteenth arrondissement, for help.

"I'll find the wire cutter myself, it'll be easier," said the former noncom. "Come back in a week."

A week later he handed me the tool. We could now proceed to the next step.

Twice a week my mother carried a parcel to Drancy. It was impossible to see the detainees because parcels were dropped off at the Red Cross barracks at the entrance, under the watchful eyes of the gendarmes. But it seemed that some of them looked the other way and, if you greased their palms a little, they let past certain forbidden items (except weapons, obviously).

To this day, I have difficulty imagining the scene: my mother, always perfectly composed and elegant, without an ounce of vulgarity or carelessness, quietly bribing a guard.

I don't know how she did it, but she did it.

We heated up the paper from the next package and learned that my father had received the wire cutter wrapped in its paper, and that it was indeed the tool he needed. Now I had to find a hideout for him and his four accomplices. I thought of my aunt who owned a studio on rue de La Michodière.

But I was quickly disabused of this idea.

"I don't want problems," she explained, a little embarrassed when I went to see her. "You understand me, right? . . ."

Oh, yes, I understood her. There were a lot of them, at that time, those who *didn't want problems.* Even when it was their own family.

I was furious when I left her. And our problems, what about them?

I then remembered a photographer in our neighborhood. He had approached me two or three days after my father was arrested to express his indignation. He, too, was a former soldier; they had no right to arrest brave men like that, for no good reason, he said. If I needed anything at all, he told me, I could count on him.

So one evening I pushed open the glass door of his shop to tell him my plan. I felt ill at ease, and my heart was beating fast. This man inspired confidence, but what was he really thinking? And what if he was afraid, or if he hadn't been sincere?

He listened to me, attentive to the end.

"Your father is a good man, an old soldier like me," he said. "I told you that you could count on me. And so now, you can count on me. Stay there."

He took down a little key hanging on a nail next to the counter and held it out to me.

"This is for you and your father. I have a studio at the rear of the courtyard. I don't use it. Come on, I'll show you."

I followed him, with a lump in my throat and my heart still thumping. The place was easily accessible. Almost too perfect. He walked me back to the exit and we shook hands.

"Be very careful, Mademoiselle," he said.

I had to make an effort to hold back my tears.

On the appointed evening, I left our apartment for Drancy before curfew set in.

Where were they all going, these people around me in the métro? For this one time I was not traveling in the last carriage. I had on dark clothing and had unstitched my yellow star. I was carrying a bag filled with a change of clothes, and I also had cash, métro tickets, and of course the key to the photographer's studio.

I arrived at Drancy about eight in the evening. Around me workers were returning home. The weather was fine, everything was calm. Dusk was falling, but I waited until it was completely dark before slipping to the spot my father had marked on a map. A few days earlier, I had already checked out the area: a narrow street sort of like a vacant lot, close to the barbed wire enclosure. I slid to the ground under some bushes, feeling like I was about to throw up.

It was eleven at night and I was drifting in and out of sleep, on high alert. If they caught me, our plan would be understood immediately. An attempt to escape, violation of curfew, failure to wear the star—I was taking a huge risk. Fortunately, no patrol passed during the night.

Papa had planned his move for around half past four in the morning, just before the curfew lifted at five. By that time workers would be out in the streets. All he and his companions would have to do was walk calmly to the métro.

The night passed slowly. Midnight, four o'clock, five o'clock. I heard Drancy waking up, birds starting to sing. A beautiful spring morning. Six o'clock, half past six, still nothing.

I finally got myself up, my head empty and my joints totally stiff. Day had returned.

I took the métro home, disheartened. If a plan that had been so well prepared had failed, nothing else was going to work. We were nowhere near to seeing father again.

My discouragement did not last long. The daily degradations, the in-justices, the acts of discrimination, the faces of sick internees from Drancy, the pale faces of Maurice and my little Bijou whom my mother was barely able to feed, the miseries of Drancy, the hostages who were shot, my father a prisoner for no reason at all, it all made me furious, in the most basic sense of the word. And what better motivator!

Like de Gaulle in London, a certain number of us no longer wanted to turn the other cheek. Anger was stronger than fear. Even so, I knew what we were risking. I saw it one day when a group of French police arrived at the hospital.

They were escorting two stretcher-bearers, who carefully set down a shape that resembled a corpse. In the room, no one said anything, and then they departed, leaving a guard at the door. I was given the signal to take care of him.

The new arrival lay on his bed in the examination room, his eyes blank, neither seeing nor hearing anything around him. He was a fright-ful sight. It was impossible to determine his age. You couldn't make out his features. His face was a mass of lacerations and wounds, his lips and eyebrows split, leaving long blackish trails of dried blood on his cheeks and down to his shoulders. A nurse came to help me. She handed me pads and disinfectant, but I didn't know where to start.

"We should undress him," she suggested, her voice tight.

It was a nightmare of a job. His shirt was in tatters and stuck to him in places with clotted blood. His body was covered with wounds and bruises. No spot had been spared. He must have had several broken ribs.

Each time we brushed against his skin, he moaned softly, but his eyes remained shut.

My heart quivering, I finished my task without him waking up.

"It's the Gestapo," Gougoutte told me that afternoon, seeing how dis-traught I was.

"He's Jewish?"

"No, not even. I really don't understand why he's here. I got the feeling the cops didn't know what to do with him. Maybe someone got the wrong message. Well, for the moment he stays here. He can't be moved."

That was a word we started to hear a lot: Gestapo, German secret police. Terrible rumors abounded about torture, beatings, disappearances. When they wanted to make you talk, they immersed you in an ice bath to the point where you thought you would die.

Some prisoners also arrived from Tourelles, the old military barracks on boulevard Mortier in the twentieth arrondissement. That's where they locked up members of the Resistance. Many came in with bad bruises, broken fingers, broken teeth. Just to see them was to imagine oneself in their place and be filled with terror.

What would have happened if I'd been discovered at Drancy? If I'd had my ribs and teeth broken, been hit in the chest or the stomach? Would I have given them the names of Monsieur Drogue, of the photographer? Would I have admitted to the invisible ink, or the gendarme bribed at the entrance? I tried to rid myself of these terrible thoughts, and to get them out of my mind altogether I assured myself that this could not happen to me.

I'd just not get caught, that's all.

The torture victim spent his first night at Rothschild without waking up.

Two days later I discovered the hospital in complete turmoil. Cops were running everywhere, from pavilion to pavilion. It was a sight I was delighted to see but it filled me with anxiety.

I asked Mademoiselle Damangout, "What's happened?"

"The patient's *disappeared*," she said, knowingly. "It's best you keep out of the way, the cops are furious."

Indeed, we could hear them interrogating people on the floor above. We quietly got ourselves out of the way and went back to work.

But the look on Gougoutte's face warmed my heart and told me in no uncertain terms that this man had not disappeared. He had escaped. And given the state he was in, he undoubtedly had accomplices inside the hospital. It was a small victory, but I didn't try to find out more about it.

I only learned the truth, or at least part of it, long after the war. The man, a Communist militant who had been arrested and beaten up by the Gestapo, had put on an act; he was just pretending to be unconscious. At the same time, he contacted Weissman, an intern who was also a Communist (I had absolutely no knowledge of this at the time), and Dupont, the pharmacist. They helped their comrade escape his second night at the hospital.

The police didn't pursue their investigation very far since they themselves were at fault. In theory, this man should never have been brought to Rothschild in the first place. So they didn't want to rock too many boats.

What they didn't know was that this escape would be the first of many.

10

The Vél d'hiv Roundup, July 16, 1942

▩ That morning avenue Hoche was radiant in the sunlight. Under a perfectly blue sky, the air was so still that the chestnut trees on either side of the street leading to the Arc de Triomphe barely stirred. To avoid seeing the red flag with its swastika flapping above the arch, I quickly descended into the métro and into the carriage for Jews. You can get used to anything, even that.

Like every day, I passed the security guards and dashed off to the changing room to put on my white coat with its yellow star, then said hello to my colleagues. Just before ten in the morning, the first rumors reached us.

"It seems they're arresting all the Jews," an intern told me at a turn in the corridor.

I smiled, doubtful, and replied, "If they are arresting all the Jews, then I should have been arrested . . . and you, too, no?"

False news was our daily bread. One day, we'd hear about the fall of Moscow, on another, it was the resignation of Pétain, and a thousand other stupidities that only thickened the fog of ignorance that surrounded us. At times we almost believed them because we liked them, or because we found them funny. More rarely, the information was actually true.

"That's not what I mean," he said. "They are arresting *all* the Jews. Men, women, and children."

This was truly incredible. This could only be a joke—an atrocious joke—but my colleague's seriousness was compelling. He wasn't the gullible kind; to the contrary, he was calm and rational.

"People are being made to pack a suitcase, then they are forced into a bus. Apparently, there are several assembly points in Paris. It's a huge roundup. There's never been one like . . ."

He stopped in mid-sentence. What did he mean? That they would round up all the Jews, even women and children? Even French Jews? If that were the case, then Maman, Maurice, and Bijou could be arrested too. My throat felt tight. But no, that was impossible. Pétain had promised to protect the French, all the French, including the Jews. And while this thought ran through my mind, I was also reminded of my father's tirades against him, the old dotard, the friend to anti-Semites.

We went back to work, our heads full of questions. If it were true, if there really were several assembly points, that in itself was a sign that the roundup was of a scale previously unheard of. In the course of the morning, there was no longer room for doubt. We learned that hundreds and hundreds of people had been arrested everywhere in Paris— the Marais, the twelfth arrondissement, the twentieth.

It was a visitor who confirmed it.

"They're taking everyone, women and children too. It seems they're being brought to the Vél d'hiv."

The rumors piled up from evidence more or less direct. The Vélodrome d'hiver was a large, indoor sports stadium in the fifteenth arrondissement of Paris, quite close to the Seine. I had never set foot inside, but I knew that that was where the famous Six Days of Paris bicycle race was held before the war. How many people were in there now? I shuddered to think. Women and children, old people. This was a terrible development. Unthinkable. This meant the Germans had been lying to us from the start. They had said they were deporting Jews to put them to work. In my great stupidity, my incurable optimism, I had wanted to believe that they were going to Brittany or Normandy to work in the fields. Then I had to accept the obvious truth: these camps were not in France, but far away toward the East. But on that day, the other truth burst into my consciousness—Jews were not leaving *in order to work.*

What kinds of work could women, children, and the elderly do? They had lied to us.

It didn't make any sense.

Another visitor told us there had been suicides. Women were said to have thrown themselves from their apartment buildings with their babies in their arms. Old people preferred to die rather than leave their homes. According to this visitor, a few policemen had quietly tipped off some families, some even the day before. Kids went into hiding, putting themselves in God's hands. Families found themselves scattered, separated in twos or threes.

The day advanced with the sun at its hottest. A good number of the thirteen thousand Jews arrested were crammed into the Vél d'hiv, piled up like old clothes to be thrown away. Breast-feeding babies, women or children on their own, old folk, men in the prime of life, women in labor, people who were sick. Thousands of lives brutally interrupted.

■ Two days later, doctors from the hospital, Didier Hesse and Marcel Leibovici, were at last allowed on the premises. They returned in the evening, exhausted and distraught. They hadn't been able to achieve anything.

"There are thousands of them," a shocked Leibovici told us. "I've never seen anything like it. . . ."

Normally, the surgery intern had a charming accent which made him roll his *r*'s. Now he stumbled over his words, his face contorted, his cheeks wet with the warm tears of a heartbroken child.

"There's nothing. They've nothing to eat, nothing to drink. They were told to take two days of food with them, but . . . I didn't think . . . Everyone's just sitting wherever they can, in the stands, or on the center lawn. Everyone's crying, women and kids. Only one tap and one toilet for everyone. Of course, they're clogged, with all these people. They're all relieving themselves everywhere, it's horrible. The smell . . . How can one . . . ? I don't understand. . . ."

Between sobs, he described the apocalypse. The glass roof made it ten times hotter, shouts echoed in a deafening racket under the thousands of light bulbs burning night and day, the appalling stench of waste, excrement. The first night they shut off the floodlights and the crowd screamed in panic, as if the nightmare had become collective, as if the anguish was contagious, the terrible anguish of death. Dozens tried to take their own lives by jumping from the highest railings. Some failed in their attempt, and there were some rather serious fractures. Children got lost in the crowd, women were giving birth on the benches, others were getting hysterical, all of this in heat like a furnace. Families stupefied by hunger, helpless old people taken away by bus who knows where. And all around were hundreds of policemen and gendarmes behind two or three barriers blocking everything.

"There were . . . I don't know how many sick people there were," said Leibovici. "Dehydration, infections, pregnant women, nervous breakdowns. Yes, there's a Red Cross tent, but no supplies. Nothing at all. What could we have done?"

He told us that some firefighters showed up, a little squad who had come to give assistance. But how could a handful of men help eight thousand people? They got out a fire hose to try to give people a little water and help them clean off some of the filth.

Then he was quiet for a long while. Several of us were crying.

"But why are they doing this?" I asked. "Why are they arresting women and kids?"

"The police said the Germans do not want to separate families. They've arrested the men. Now they're arresting everyone at the same time."

Four days after these events, we saw the first patients arrive at the hospital. Another shock, a violent one. There were around twenty of them; some were children, but mostly they were very old people, dehydrated and dying. Unable to walk any longer, they came in on stretchers, almost comatose and repulsively filthy.

I was given the care of an elderly couple, both unconscious. I realized right away that nothing could be done for them. Why then had they been arrested, these two? Why lock them up, send them to another country? What wrongs had they committed?

I tried to give them a few sips of water.

"Open your mouth, Monsieur. That's it. Open your mouth."

A nurse helped me by holding his head, but it was pointless. He did not have the strength to drink.

"This isn't working," the nurse whispered. "Perhaps we should try a tonic?" The old man's features were blank. He smelled of sweat, grime, his clothes were soiled.

His hands were those of a laborer, gnarled with arthritis, with a bluish tinge. Where had he come from? Poland, Russia, Romania like my grandfather Abraham? I gritted my teeth and tried not to think of him.

I sought some advice from a doctor who was navigating a path between beds that were tightly packed together for the survivors of this shipwreck.

"I don't know. Maybe try an enema, that might get a bit of fluid in him."

Seeing my alarm, he understood my concern immediately and grimaced with an air of helplessness.

"Well, try all the same to get him to drink a little something. And a bit of Coramine, too, if you can find any."

He went back to his work. His department was inundated. He had his own emergencies.

I rushed around to find this drug, a stimulant for the heart. The dose was insufficient, but that's all I could get. The nurse helped me give it to him in a glass of water. We ended up spilling three quarters of it.

I felt utterly useless, with a great urge to sob and scream at the same time.

He and his wife no longer had the strength to swallow anything. Over the next day or so, I watched them decline.

Then they died, as did some others.

▪ The Vélodrome d'hiver roundup* gave rise to public protests. Some priests and bishops spoke out from the pulpit: things were going too far with the Jews, they are our brothers. Have we forgotten all charity, all Christian morality?

*On July 16–17, 1942, French police arrested 13,152 Jews, including 4,051 children. More than 6,000 of them were interned in the Vélodrome d'hiver until they were sent to other camps in France, and eventually deported. It was France's largest mass arrest of Jews. For decades, the French government denied willing cooperation with the occupier. On the fifty-third anniversary of the roundup, July 16, 1995, President Jacques Chirac at last acknowledged France's active participation in the Holocaust and apologized. With respect to the Vel d'hiv, he said, "France, land of the Enlightenment and Human Rights, land of hospitality and asylum, France, on that day, committed an irreparable act. It failed to keep its word and delivered those under its protection to their executioners." On July 16, 2017, President Emmanuel Macron added, "It is indeed France that organized this roundup, . . . not a single German took part."

Most Jews understood what was happening, especially the foreign Jews for whom memories of pogroms were fresher: the Germans had shifted into high gear. Many sought to flee or hide by any means possible. The French Jews were more reluctant; some believed they were safe, protected by our great Marshal. They lived openly, displaying the star almost proudly, absurdly confident vis-à-vis these people who so obviously hated us.

From Drancy, my father had watched the tragedy unfold. He saw these families arrive, these women, these children. For him it was clear: it was time for us to flee.

Here, I must step back a little in time.

After the night I spent in the vacant lot next to Drancy, I went home in despair and above all riddled with anxiety. What had happened? Why had my father not come? Had he been denounced? Deported? Taken hostage and shot?

For a few days, we imagined the worst. Maman sent a parcel with the usual message in invisible ink, and we got the answer back. He was alive and well, like always.

Everything had been ready, he explained to us, he and his companions had decided to act at the agreed-upon time. But at the last moment their plan fell apart. As they were leaving their barracks room, a little before dawn, they were stopped by the other prisoners who didn't want trouble. And although my father tried to convince them, there was no way: the fear of reprisals was too strong. If he and his companions insisted on trying to escape, the others would alert the gendarmes.

So they stayed put, with heavy hearts.

It was a bitter pill to swallow, but I was relieved all the same to know that Papa had not yet been deported. So there was still a chance, even though I believed it less and less.

But from his prison, he insisted we should flee. He got word to Maman through the usual channel:

Don't worry about me anymore, leave, all of you. Go to Yoyo, where she is. I'll figure something out.

Where Yoyo was, was Tunis.

I looked at my mother. The wrapping paper was shaking in my trembling hands. Without exchanging a word, we all agreed: obeying father was out of the question. At bottom, we Brulls were all alike—stubborn as mules.

"I really am going to get him out," she said again and again, as if repeating this would make it true. "Georges Lamirand is a good guy. He has always liked your father. He is one of his former students. He said he would help us and I am sure he will. We have to try."

Maurice gravely nodded his head, Bijou too. We had to stay. And I was one hundred percent in agreement. Besides we had no money, so where could we go? It was also very dangerous. Many Jews fleeing south were caught trying to cross the line of demarcation. They ended up in internment camps and were then deported.

◾ After the Vélodrome d'hiver roundup, the rhythm of transports to the East accelerated. Trains left from Drancy (and perhaps from the camps in the Loiret) almost every day. And they carried everyone: women, infants, adults, the elderly. It had all been so carefully planned. We were caught in a net, turning around and around in panic, trapped in the invisible mesh.

Some nights seemed filled with menace as I tried to fall asleep. I no longer felt safe anywhere. The building was silent, but I knew that if we heard even the faintest sound of footsteps on the stairs, we would all leap up. I feared identity checks in the métro, identity checks at the hospital, identity checks at Drancy. I feared for Papa. Maurice was no longer safe going to school, nor was Bijou even though she spent her days at home, and nor was Maman when she went searching for food.

Fear was our companion. It followed us step by step and tightened its grip more and more every day.

At the lab in the evenings, we exchanged scraps of information about these convoys, this constant threat.

"They have roll calls for the next departure. Those whose names are on the list have to pack their bags," explained Gougoutte, who had a pass for Drancy. "They are isolated in a separate area overnight. The next day they are assembled in the courtyard, counted, and put onto buses. Then they are taken to the train station at Bourget, but not the one for regular travelers. There's a marshaling yard a little farther down. There they are counted again."

"And we still don't know where they are going?" I asked.

"No. The SS tell them that they are going to work in the East and that there will be reprisals if anyone escapes. Then they are shoved in, at least fifty to a wagon meant for forty. Sometimes even more: sixty, eighty! Apparently there are no openings anywhere. And the trains leave in the morning."

We looked at each other in horror. The conditions for the voyage were appalling: there were only two buckets in each wagon, one filled with water, the other for everyone's needs. Gougoutte could not find out if any food was distributed at the departure, but we could guess. And we didn't believe that the deportees would be treated any better once they arrived.

I murmured, "The women and children are separated?"

Her eyes filled with tears. She shook her head.

"Everyone is mixed in together—women, children, old people. They are squeezed in so tightly that no one is able to sit down. And the voyage lasts two or three days. . . . At least if it's Poland, as they are saying . . ."

"That's awful . . ."

"Yes . . . Yes, it's awful. Nothing we can do about it."

The Germans were lying to us. Why were we setting fractures, treating ulcers and appendicitis attacks, why were we helping women give birth and caring for the little old folks, just so they'd be treated like this?

What use was the hospital?

For a long moment no one spoke. Many of us had family or friends in Drancy. For me, it was my father. Each morning at roll call, he must be shaking inside. One day, perhaps he would hear his name. . . .

An unbearable thought, but I was powerless to do anything about it.

The only place I could act was here at the hospital: delay the return of patients to Drancy for as long as possible. Maybe I would not be able to save my father, but I might save others.

By any means.

Now we were ready to act.

11

Disappearances

■ The pressure on Rothschild continued to intensify. We were an annex of Drancy, as we were constantly reminded. The Germans weren't playing around with the hospital; it really got under their skin. For them all sick Jews were malingerers. For some months, a fanatical Nazi had been running Drancy, a certain Dannecker.* He starved the detainees to the point of death. And he systematically opposed any hospitalization, even for those who were dying.

He had the pavilions holding internees fenced in with barbed wire. He regularly demanded their return to Drancy—it was an obsession with him. One day, when he ordered that six out of every ten sick internees be sent back, the director tried to resist him. Dannecker insisted, spitting out in his staccato French that any unjustified and prolonged stay would have grave consequences for the patients as well as the hospital staff.

And these were not idle threats.

One evening after work, I ran into Leibovici in the duty room. He looked devastated and could barely stand up. All day long there had been rumors about Dannecker visiting the hospital. He confirmed them, and with good reason: he had been in the crosshairs.

*Theodor Dannecker, SS captain, deputy to Adolf Eichmann and Reinhard Heydrich, was in charge of the Jewish question in France from September 1940 to August 1942.

"The guy's the caricature of a Nazi," he said to me, his voice still hoarse: impeccable dark uniform, tall leather riding boots, death's head cap, and most of all, that kind of imbecilic fury, always screaming. He arrived in the morning, unannounced and accompanied by an interpreter. He was already hysterical.

"He's a madman," said Leibovici, still terror-struck. "A madman in a uniform." The first thing he did was slap the cop at the guard post, who didn't protest, obviously, and that spoke volumes about how servile we'd become.

"I was in the courtyard," said Leibo. "He walked right up to me and kicked me with those boots!"

I looked at him, aghast.

"Yes, kicked me. I hadn't done anything, I hadn't even seen him. He asked to see my department, so I took him there. He followed me, shrieking like a polecat. When we got to surgery, he demanded to see the chief, but you know H. . . . ."

My face showed I knew where this was going.

"Of course he told me he couldn't come and that I'd have to show Dannecker around myself. The first case he saw was a guy missing an arm, a veteran of 1914. He had draped his jacket over his shoulders, his jacket with the Légion d'honneur on it. Dannecker started to howl and cuffed him around the ear twice, knocking him down. Then he insisted on seeing all the patients, one by one. I showed him an appendicitis case. 'She's healed, that one! She has to go back to Drancy.' He was screaming. 'But the lady's just been operated on. It's only been two days.' 'So what! My secretary was operated on for her appendix, too. Eight days later, she was back at work.' And with that he tore off her dressing. 'There, now she's healed. Send her back to Drancy.' So I was forced to put her back on the list. Further on was a man who'd just had a stomach operation two days before. Dannecker yelled even louder:

'So what! You can live without a stomach. *A Jew can live without a stomach!*'"

Leibovici paused for a few seconds, his throat was dry. As for myself, I had a hard time believing that this was all true, that this had really happened here, in a hospital. The entire visit had been a nightmare, Dannecker more and more furious with each step.

"Then, at one point, I came to a patient from whom I'd removed a ganglion. He asked me what that was. I had an inspiration and replied, 'Tuberculosis.' He kicked me away, as if the bacillus was about to land on his face. I almost fell over. 'Get away, dirty Jew! Step back.' I had found the solution. We went to the ward on the floor above and there, they were all tuberculosis cases. Funny, huh?"

Leibo managed a slight grin, and I did, too. The rest was not so funny. Undoubtedly enraged by this sudden outbreak of tuberculosis (the Germans were deathly afraid of contagious diseases), Dannecker ended his visit, staring hard at him.

Then he took out his pistol and pointed it at him. Without a word. Again the intern's voice began to shake.

"I really thought he was going to kill me," he whispered. "I felt as though I was tied to a stake. He looked at me like I was already dead, I saw it in his eyes. Then he slowly backed out of the room, as if he was still going to shoot me. When he was finally gone for good, the patients got up from their beds to come kiss my hand. 'Why? I did nothing,' I told them. 'Because Dannecker's crazy. At Drancy he sometimes takes out his revolver and kills one or two of us, just like that, for nothing.'"

The day after the visit, a police vehicle arrived, filled with armed policemen. There were several dozen patients on Dannecker's list, some crippled, pale, some still burning with fever. They were taken back to Drancy. The prisoners from the barracks at Tourelles were sent somewhere else, no one knew where. And now, in some of the departments, all the beds were empty.

"Even the cops had tears in their eyes," said a witness to the scene. "They had to help the patients climb into the vans."

Three weeks later, Samy Halfon, the director, vanished too. Seeing I was worried about him, Gougoutte told me he was being held at Drancy.

"During his visit, Dannecker demanded information from him about the patients," she said. "He refused to answer, invoking professional confidentiality. It seems that Dannecker was screaming so loudly he could be heard in the courtyard. When Halfon was summoned to Drancy, some people told him not to go, but he went anyway."

Leibovici had better luck.

Some time later, while examining a patient, he received a call from the switchboard operator, telling him that two policemen had just passed through the main entrance and were coming for him in his pavilion. Leibo dropped everything and went down to the basement where an underground corridor led to the other buildings, and to the exit. That was the last we saw of him.

■ I felt I was living a nightmare. Outwardly, nothing had changed at the hospital, except for the barbed wire. But it had been transformed into something hideous, as if the horror that had begun in Poland— some of us could smell it—had reached here and was seeping into our buildings, into our souls.

Yet, here was the hospital, right in the middle of the city, in plain sight. And no one had a clue.

One evening, around the time of the Vél d'hiv roundup, I arrived home to find a couple, both dentists, that my parents used to see before the war. For despite the deprivations and our poverty, my mother continued to put on a good show and entertain people. Our lives had not stopped.

"Is something the matter, Mademoiselle? You seem upset," the woman said to me.

Just the way she put the question made me furious. But honestly, how could they know what I had seen? So, in a lackluster voice, I took it upon myself to tell them what I had witnessed. My mother listened gravely. But they, they shook their heads in disbelief. Naïvely, I had thought they would be deeply shocked, like I was.

After a short silence, after I'd stopped talking, the woman spoke up.

"Goodness, Mademoiselle, really . . . Deporting sick people? Are you sure you're not exaggerating just a bit?"

I stared at her darkly as if I had just been slapped. How dare she not believe me?

My mother made a gesture as if to say to calm down, but I took no notice.

"No, I am not exaggerating," I said, matter-of-factly. "These people are in no state to be deported. I am an intern. I know. But they *are* being deported. That is what's happening."

There they sat, he in a smart suit, well-dressed, not a care in the world, with his little round tummy, she with her jewels and curls, her plump cheeks and painted lips. Calm and smug, blind and stupid.

"Come on," said the husband. "This is nonsense. You're not going to make me believe that, Mademoiselle."

He smiled at me, with a hint of condescension. Taken aback, I was struck dumb, so I turned on my heel and left.

■ Every morning, I left for the hospital with fear in the pit in my stomach and the feeling I was going to do battle with monsters. If someone had given me a bomb, I would not have hesitated to throw it at the Germans, and too bad if I blew up with it. But nobody did. So for lack of bombs, I fought in my own fashion.

Never mind that Drancy continued to reclaim its sick internees and that the Germans and their collabos continued to spy on us, we kept inventing new ways to lie to them, to rob them of the men and women they wanted to deport, to devour.

We altered diagnoses, found complications where there were none, detected tuberculosis cases. After all, the SS were not doctors. And for neophytes, what was more unreadable than a lung X-ray?

In surgery—unbeknownst to H. who continued to be scared to death—we operated on certain detainees who were already healed. For instance, one resistance fighter in perfect health had her appendix removed. To no avail: she was deported a few days later before a way was found for her to escape during her convalescence.

We had to save the babies, the ones in maternity, and they were many.

The chief of maternity, Dr. Walther, had obtained from the former director an agreement that mothers could remain at the hospital for six months to breastfeed their infants. I learned that an abnormally high number of stillborn births were being recorded.

They had been declared stillborn, but they were very much alive.

All this took place in the utmost secrecy. I suppose that someone approached these mothers and explained to them that their babies could be saved from being deported, but that in order to do this, they'd have to give them up. Most mothers probably accepted despite their heartbreak. Who would not do this for their child? We found them safe havens, families. They would not be put on the trains.

The babies left for destinations unknown.

Rumor had it that they left at night through the morgue door on rue Santerre, which was not guarded and opportunely left unlocked.

That morgue door through which I, too, eventually passed.

12

The Children

▪ On the day of the roundup I saw a few small children come in, sick with measles or diphtheria. One of them, a little boy, wore an enormous bandage around his head that made him look like an Easter egg with a forced smile.

I tried to ask him a few questions but got no response.

"It's because of a woman at the Vél d'hiv," the nurse told me. "She went completely crazy and hit him on the head over and over with a broken bottle. His face was covered with blood, the poor kid. He hasn't said a word since he arrived. I believe that his parents are in a camp in the Loiret."

How old was this kid? Three years old, four?

Preoccupied with other tasks, I no longer looked in on him. Sometimes, from a turn in the hallway, I saw him sitting on his bed. The bandages got smaller and he seemed to regain his strength and color. And then one day he was gone. Had he been returned to his parents?

Was it possible that certain children just disappeared, like the newborns in maternity? That was the burning question, but I didn't want to ask Gougoutte. If he had been smuggled out, there was no need for me to know.

One day, I remarked to her, as if inadvertently, that we didn't see the child with the head wounds anymore.

A look of uncertainty came over her face, as if she were trying to recall him.

"Oh, that kid? I don't know. I guess he got better?"

She gave me a vague smile and walked away. I was flustered. If he had been sent back to his parents, to their camp in the Loiret, she would not have made that face, for sure. If she didn't trust me, her answer would have been much more evasive, something like: "I'm not familiar with his case. . . . He wasn't in my department."

From her reaction, I guessed he'd been removed from the hospital, and not in order to return to Drancy: he was outside, free. Exactly how, she didn't have to tell me. But I concluded there was a system, an organization.

Two or three days after the roundup, I noticed a little girl, about two and a half years old, alone in her iron-barred crib, mute, her eyes wide, watching the adults who passed by without seeing her. Our eyes met and instantly I was reminded of Bijou, when the two of us were together in Tunisia.

She was very pale and remained perfectly still, like someone afraid of bothering people, of drawing attention to herself.

I asked her her name.

"Danielle," she said in a voice that was almost inaudible.

For a child of her age, she expressed herself rather well, but very timidly, her big eyes filled with incomprehension and with all the horrible things she must have seen at the Vél d'hiv.

I learned from a nurse that she had been arrested with both her parents and her older sister, who had been taken to Drancy without her.

"But you are going to see them again, you know. Do you hurt anywhere?"

The little girl shook her head in silence. Then she coughed a little, her eyes feverish.

"In here, there's nothing to be afraid of. You'll see, everyone will take good care of you. I'm sure you'll see your Maman and Papa again soon."

As I said these words, I tried to look confident, but my heart ached. Deep down, I knew it would be better if she never saw her parents again. If she did, that would mean she'd been sent to Drancy and would be put on the next convoy with them. To see her parents and sister again, that's surely what she was hoping for, but we had to avoid this at any cost.

I raised my hand to her forehead, a little abruptly I'm afraid, because she flung herself backwards, her eyes wide as if I might strike her. She was shaking all over. Very gently, I took hold of her fingers. There was something terribly sad in this odd conversation of ours, maybe because this child had touched my heart, and because I sensed I was going to love her without being able to stop myself.

She was in shock, very weak, dehydrated. Ever since her arrival, she had refused to speak, and I was the only person to whom she had said anything.

I promised her I'd come back and see her.

As time went on, Danielle gradually came back to life. She regained some energy and started to speak normally again. At first confined to her pavilion, she started to go outside, even though the chill of autumn was beginning to set in. No one really kept an eye on her, and after a few weeks, she wandered up and down the paths between the pavilions, like a child adopted by the hospital.

It was a strange situation, and I sometimes wondered how the Germans were not aware of it. They wanted to shut us in, without realizing that the walls would also shield us from their prying eyes.

Within a few weeks, the little girl knew my first name, and those of all the doctors and nurses. She was quite small, dark-haired like Bijou, a laugh like crystal, and the deliberate but awkward gait of a child for whom the world is immense. Everything she did reminded me most deeply of the child I once was. Her innocence, her purity. Her absolute disregard for what tomorrow might bring.

When she saw me coming, she'd greet me, showing me that for her I was someone special, that nothing could come between us, that we would be friends forever. I always managed to bring her something, a little piece of cake when possible, rediscovering the habits I'd had with Bijou, those little games that made us laugh so much.

In every child I have cared for since, I have rediscovered her face, that pure confidence and naïve certainty that adults would love and help you. Every one of these moments is etched in my being.

I was not the only one to grow attached to Danielle, who had become in some respects our mascot, the hospital's child, our pride, living proof that we were doing more than our job, that in our own fashion we were fouling up the Nazi machine. More and more, she began to leave the prisoners' ward. She wasn't the only one: by now there were seven or eight children permanently with us. Some of them, the smallest, were sometimes taken for buggy rides around the hospital. But Danielle was special. The nurses and interns, even the cops at the gate, gave her things to eat, played and joked around with her.

And so it happens that there are children who know how to talk to adults.

■ One day, I received permission to take her out, just for an afternoon. I had to bring her back before dinner, without fail. I took her aside to get her dressed.

She let herself be dressed like a little rag doll, her arms raised to the sky. "Where are we going?"

"I'm taking you to my home. You'll see, I have a sister, her name is Sonia, but we call her Bijou. Everyone calls her Bijou."

"Is she as big as Céline?"

Céline was her big sister, five years old, still interned with her parents in Drancy. "No, she's even bigger, almost ten years old. But you'll see, she's very nice. Stand up straight so I can do up your coat."

"She's ten?"

Danielle seemed a bit dreamy, as though being ten years old was an astonishing feat, almost unimaginable.

And so we set out, the two of us, hand in hand. To take the métro, we had to walk along rue Santerre to the Bel-Air station and climb up steps that were a bit too steep for her. We got into the last carriage reserved for Jews, then on with our ride. Danielle asked simple questions about the people, about the gray sky above us in the above-ground parts of the métro, about the noise of the rails and the carriage doors. She pretended to be frightened of the noise the train made in the tunnel, and we laughed. And I answered her childish questions without thinking too much.

We had a snack at the house, just a bite. She met my mother and played with Bijou for part of the afternoon. Later we took the métro back, together, hand in hand.

During the ride, I watched the stations go by and smelled the thick stink of the long tunnels. I wasn't the only adult with children. Without my star, no one would have noticed us, and I said to myself that I could continue on to the railway station, get on a train going south, escape with the little girl, cross the line and find her a family. Then come back.

Ridiculous ideas that passed in a flash. I had promised Gougoutte to bring Danielle back to the hospital. And Gougoutte answered for me to Claire Heyman, the social worker. I couldn't betray them, there would be reprisals. And besides, where would I go with this toddler and not a franc on me.

And what would become of Maman, Maurice and Bijou, and Papa? We went back to Rothschild, and I went home, alone.

A few weeks later, Céline, her five-year-old big sister, was admitted to the hospital with constant sore throats. Nothing too serious and she soon recovered. But we kept her here with her sister all the same.

They were better off here than at Drancy.

Between shifts, I continued to take care of Danielle, as I had done with Bijou. I was her little mother, I loved her laughter, her innocence, her questions, and the way she smiled at me and held her arms out to me. I loved all of her, as one does with a child of almost three. And I observed her progress, proudly, tenderly, as if she were my own little daughter.

13

Going Underground

■ The summer of 1942 ended quietly.

In our secret exchanges on parcel wrapping (parcels that became ever lighter as we grew ever poorer), Papa begged us to return to Tunisia with Bijou and Maurice and leave him to fend for himself.

Out of the question, even though the thought sometimes crossed my mind that staying was madness, that hope was for naught, and that he would never get out. At other times, I told myself that we had no right to give up. And if fate would have it that he was deported, we could always then try to flee by whatever means we could.

His letters left me horribly sad. I felt guilty about his failed escape, even if it was not my fault. Fortunately, my mother's fierce determination reinforced my own when mine wavered. But her beautiful face had grown pale, she looked exhausted, spending most of her time looking for something to feed the three of us.

"Any news from Georges Lamirand?"

"I wrote him at the beginning of the month. He told me he's doing everything he can. But you know . . . He's a minister, he must be busy."

I had to agree, kind of.

"True, he's busy, but he said he would help Papa. I'm sure he will."

"Of course he will. We just need to wait."

There was nothing more to say. We both knew very well that Papa would not be able to stay in his barracks room forever, waiting out the roll calls. One day he too would walk down to the courtyard with his little suitcase and climb into a wagon like everyone else.

That was clear.

Just before the new school term, we were hit with some bad news—or rather, even more bad news, but who was counting?

"The principal of Louis-le-Grand* has asked to see me about Maurice," my mother told me. "Something about his behavior, but that's all I know. I can't go, I have to go find some butter. Or at least some margarine."

Finding meat or eggs was a real feat at that time, a Herculean combat, and I admired her grit. It meant hours in line, often for nothing, followed by the quest for the Holy Grail on the black market for a small fortune.

So I went off to the lycée in her stead.

Maurice was in his next to last year at Louis-le-Grand, in the heart of the Latin Quarter. I arrived at the school at the top of rue Saint-Jacques a bit anxious, for up to now he had always been a good student, he didn't misbehave. What drama was about to unfold?

The principal's office was upstairs in the majestic white stone building, overlooking a courtyard of chestnut trees. Now, at the end of the summer holidays, the quiet was absolute, broken only by birdsong. The principal received me very politely, closing the door behind us after a final look around.

"So, you are the big sister," he said, after looking me up and down very carefully, with particular attention to the yellow star on my chest.

I said yes.

---

*Louis-le-Grand, one of the most prestigious and rigorous secondary schools in Paris, founded 1563. Among its alumni were presidents Giscard d'Estaing, Pompidou, and Chirac, and the writers Molière, Hugo, and Sartre.

"Naturally, Mademoiselle, all this must stay strictly between us," (he lowered his voice, glancing occasionally at his office door). "I have to tell you that we are completely satisfied with your brother's conduct..."

I did not have time to voice my astonishment.

"...but I absolutely had to tell you. We have some information.... Very well, let me give this to you straight: we don't think it's a good idea for your brother to return at the beginning of the term."

"But . . . for how long?"

"I don't know, Mademoiselle," he said, interlacing his fingers, looking apologetic. "It would be . . . wise if he didn't come back for at least several weeks. Do you understand?"

I understood all too well. We heard here and there about certain students disappearing. Either they were in hiding with their families, or they'd been arrested. Certainly we saw fewer and fewer yellow stars in the streets.

From then on, Maurice stayed home all day with Bijou, who was also deprived of school. Seventeen-year-old brother and nine-year-old sister shut in, terrified they'd never see the adults come home, terrified they'd hear police climb the stairs and knock at the door.

The two of them built for themselves a world of dreams, of boredom and fear. Of hunger, too, because we had practically no silver left to sell and the food ration coupons barely sufficed. Maurice was already tall, with sunken cheeks and shining eyes; Bijou would look at me, uncomprehending. All we adults talked about was disasters and threats.

My brother had explored the neighborhood, with the intention of showing Bijou the route she should take if ever Maman and I disappeared, and if the Germans came for them.

"First of all, if someone rings the bell, don't answer."

"Even if it's Maman?"

"Maman has keys and Colette has keys. If someone rings the bell, that means it's someone else. So don't answer, OK? Come with me."

Maurice led the way, the tall, skinny adolescent, followed by his sister, slender and silent. He went out to the back stairs, which opened into the kitchen.

"You go down this way, and don't forget to shut the door behind you before you go down, do you understand?"

"Yes."

"OK, repeat what I've just said."

"I leave, I shut the door, and then I go down the stairs."

"That's right. If you leave the door open, they'll see right away that that's the way you left, and they'll follow you and catch you. If it's shut, they won't know and you'll have plenty of time."

"Yes, I get it. But anyway, you'll be with me, right?"

"Maybe. But not necessarily. If I'm not here, don't wait for me. Get out. Leave without me if I'm not here. I'll manage on my own."

He showed her how to escape through the cellar. You had to make your way through rows of recesses in the dark, in the dust, with faint rays of sunlight filtering through narrow openings only every so often. Then you came out into a courtyard and could go into the apartment building across the way, where there lived a woman who seemed kind and maybe would help Bijou. And if she didn't want to, or wasn't in, then there were friends in Paris who would take her.

Regularly, they retraced the escape route. Bijou walked behind him slowly, warily.

"But what if there are rats?"

"There are no rats."

"Yes, there are."

"They'll be afraid of you."

"And the spiders, too?"

"The spiders, too."

"Yes, and if you're not with me?"

"Don't worry, I'll be there. But if I'm not, my spirit will guide you."

She looked at him in alarm.

"My spirit will guide you, you will follow the route I've shown you, you *will* be able to do it without me. You'll see, you won't be afraid."

▪ But Maurice left earlier than planned, and Bijou never needed this escape route. Because there was Father Kenneth.

We had met this unusual person a few months earlier. Around fifty, very tall, with bright blue eyes and attractive features, he vaguely resembled an American actor; he spoke with a very marked accent, and for good reason: he was Irish.

Very quickly, we conversed in his native tongue.

"My name is Kenneth Monaghan," he said to me, "But they call me Father Kenneth. I am the priest at Saint Joseph's Church, next door. I am a friend of your father's. I know he's been interned in Drancy. You must be Colette."

Guardedly, I responded in the affirmative. The fact that he knew all these details didn't make him a friend. And his clothing intrigued me. I was sure that all priests wore a cassock, so why was he in civilian clothing, and well dressed at that?

Ignoring my reticence, he assured me of his support. The church was just next to our apartment; we could seek his help whenever we wished. He would show up from time to time, like a good neighbor, chat with me and Maman, ask for news of my father, and then be off again.

One day, Maman told him that Maurice could no longer attend school. The Irish priest thought it over for a few moments.

"He is not safe here." (His accent really could be cut with a knife.) "You know, I may have a way to get him into the Free Zone. Do you know where you could send him, down there? Do you have some safe place he could go?"

My mother's face tensed up. She told Maurice and Bijou to go to their rooms. The less they knew for the time being, the better for everyone. Instinctively, we had all gone underground.

Once we were alone with Father Kenneth, she replied, "My family in Tunisia could take him."

He was silent for a moment, looking frankly first at me, and then at my mother. "That should work. So all we have to do is get him to Marseille, where he can get a ticket for Tunis. On the other hand, he'll need money for the boat."

"And . . . for the smugglers? I've heard that some of them charge a lot."

"These ones won't want money."

Reassured, my mother hesitated for a moment, then asked about Bijou. Father Kenneth shook his head, regretfully.

"She's too young. You have to walk a very long way to cross the line of demarcation. These are smugglers' routes. She'd never be able to follow them."

My mother's face froze. I could see she was holding back her tears, tears of both sadness and relief.

One morning, a few days later, Maurice waited in the living room with his little rucksack, a clandestine traveler. I can still recall his face, pale but resolute, that nervous fragility of teenage boys. My mother held him tightly, her eyes red, trying not to cry again.

"It'll be all right, Maman. You're going to get through this. Colette is here. And then Papa . . . He'll find a way to get out."

His voice was unsteady, his lips trembled a bit and his fingers too, as he gripped mother's shoulder.

"Yes. Of course he'll find a way. Of course things will work out. As for you, take care of yourself. Be careful about everything. I put a sandwich in the pocket of your rucksack. Some water too. Be careful with your money. Above all, don't show it to anyone and don't talk about it."

"You've already told me that, Maman, don't worry. It'll be fine, I'm not stupid."

She looked at him again, then put her arms around him once more.

We heard him go down the stairs. Then he was off down the street, a thin silhouette among the bare trees.

That evening, the apartment felt strange. We ate in silence, the clattering of our forks loud in the poorly lit room.

Paris plunged into the blackout. Soon we would hear the marching boots of German patrols. There might be an alert, with sirens and the sounds of bombs farther away in the working-class suburbs. We quickly finished our meager meal. Bijou asked no questions; she clearly understood that her big brother would not be sleeping here, not this night nor any other.

Now we were just two women and a little girl. Alone in the world.

■ At the laboratory, we spent long evenings with Gougoutte, sorting out fake news from real news.

"The Germans say they're going to take Stalingrad," said Simon Schwartz. "But Radio London is saying they won't be taking anything."

"I say that the boches have not yet had their last word. It seems they've destroyed one of his armies again, I don't know which one."

Simon rolled his eyes.

"One of his armies? So what difference does that make to Stalin? He has other armies!"

"Maybe, Monsieur Schwartz. But I am telling you that as of now, all he has done, your Stalin, is retreat. And let me also point out that the Volga and Stalingrad are four thousand kilometers from Paris. We're not going to be seeing them any time soon, your Russians."

"Nor your Americans."

"The fact remains, the Americans have started to bomb Germany. They're reporting it on Radio London. The boches are keeping quiet about it. Still, it's something."

That winter the whole world was watching Stalingrad. Germans suffering, that delighted us, that's the horror of war. The newsreels may have shown us the German troops crushing the Bolshevik hordes, waving their white mittens and smiling wide, but the city still did not fall. And we prayed it never would.

■ In that endless night, sometimes the news was good: a few weeks after his departure, we received a postcard from Maurice, safely arrived in Tunis.

■ Then, in November, when we were least expecting it, we received another extraordinary piece of news. Papa's friend Georges Lamirand, the Pétainist, had kept his word: my father was going to be released.

My mother was transfigured, but I couldn't believe it. Every day I saw how relentlessly the Germans were deporting the Jews. Until he was actually in the house, I would not believe it.

A few days later, Papa pushed open the apartment door. He looked like a ghost. Eleven months had passed, but he looked as though it had been years. His face was ashen, gaunt, and every small step left him breathless. He wore a coat with sleeves so threadbare you would have thought he'd fought a tramp over it. Only his eyes were unchanged, black and fierce, ablaze with intelligence. His appearance shocked us.

He was like an old man. Even Bijou, who had been hopping about all week with impatience, froze with shock.

Once the surprise—the bad part of the surprise—wore off, we threw ourselves, all three of us, into his arms, overwhelmed with emotion, our cheeks flooded with tears, unable to speak for a long while. Suddenly, a strange sensation came over me, that none of this was going to last, that perhaps things were going too well.

We lingered in conversation for a long time after dinner. His voice seemed to me weaker than I remembered, and I found it hard to get used to his deeply furrowed cheeks, but his will and his authority were intact, even strengthened by these long months of suffering. As was his habit, he did not dwell on what he had lived through himself and first wanted to hear about Maurice.

When we told him, he seemed intensely relieved.

"Father Kenneth is a good man. I was sure of him, but one never knows what might have happened. Anyway, it's over now, and that's good."

"There's still Bijou . . ."

"I know. We'll find a way," he answered, placing his hand on my mother's. The contact made her jump.

"Bijou cannot stay here, but I'll find something. I'll need a little time, but I'll get there."

Then he asked me how my work was going at the hospital, and if I planned on staying there. Almost annoyed, I stared at him in surprise.

"Why? I shouldn't stay?"

"It's getting dangerous. It forces you to go out every day with your star. With all these roundups . . . You know, Colette, I was released, but it was a miracle. It won't happen again. Georges Lamirand has enemies in the government. He won't stay a minister forever. If I am arrested again, or if you are captured, I'm afraid there won't be anyone left to help us."

"What do you want me to do then? Stay here all day? Give up school and my position as an intern?"

"No, Colette, of course not."

He gave me a sorry smile, more like a grimace, and changed the subject.

He rested for a little more than a week, then started to go out *to see friends*. Even if he weren't my father, I would have noticed how quickly he now became short of breath. His pace had always been brisk, an athlete flying up the stairs almost at a run; now he climbed haltingly, one slow step after the other. Internment had affected him more than he was willing to admit, he who in his letters from Drancy had always maintained he was in *perfect health*. One evening that week, I found my mother's worried face from our worst days had returned. She was yelling at Bijou and pacing nervously.

My father, sitting in his armchair, watched me come in without saying a word. He was waxy pale, his nose was pinched.

"What's wrong?" I said, with a lump in my throat.

"Nothing. It'll pass."

"For someone who has nothing wrong, you don't look too good."

He finally admitted that for some time he had been feeling rather sharp pains in his chest.

"You had them in Drancy?"

"Not often. I think I'm just a bit tired. They go away if I rest."

He tried to smile at me, but I was not fooled. In my year as an intern, I had learned to see when a man was suffering. It just took me a second to read the distress in his eyes, but at the same time the strength of a

man who would never give up. He was tired, very unwell, exhausted for
sure. At that thought, I abruptly turned my head away with a terrible
urge to cry, like a little girl who understands that her father will die.

All the while, Maman walked around the apartment, doing or un-
doing I don't know what, and nagging poor Bijou, as if she could do
anything about it.

He told me that since Drancy, he had experienced chest pain, in other
words, angina. He could have a heart attack at any moment. I said nothing. There was no treatment, aside from rest.

But my father had absolutely no intention of taking it easy. He considered himself a soldier at war.

Pretty soon, he called us together one evening to outline the plan he
had put in motion:

"I've contacted a friend, Monsieur Dekeukelaere. He has a factory
in Courtrai, in Belgium."

We immediately understood what he meant. Maman turned very
pale, her lips white from holding back her tears, but she got hold of herself, always dignified and proud.

"He has a daughter exactly the same age as Bijou. He's ready to take
her until the war is over. He'll say that she's his niece."

"But . . . when?"

"As soon as we can. That is, if you agree, of course. Dekeukelaere is
perfect. She will be safe there. That is what you wanted, isn't it?"

My mother, her gaze vacant, did not answer right away. Great tears
ran down to her lips, but she paid them no heed. Rarely had I seen her
suffer like that, and I felt my eyes stinging, too. Bijou . . .

"Yes, of course, that's better."

"What's more, Dekeukelaere works for the Germans. It's the perfect
hiding place. They'll never guess."

"And . . . when?"

"As soon as possible. He comes often to Paris, he has an *Ausweis*, a pass. I need to get counterfeit papers for Bijou, but don't worry, everything will be fine. It's better like that, don't you think?"

My mother's face twisted in pain and she began to weep, deep violent sobs that shook her shoulders, a bottomless grief that nothing could assuage. And though I understood the danger of having Bijou stay with us, the horror of those trains, I was, like my mother, overcome with grief.

With Maurice, it had been different. He was almost an adult, and then he was going to join our family in Tunisia. But Bijou . . . She was only nine, she was going to be alone in a foreign country, in the home of people she had never met.

I cast my mind back to that time in Tunis, when she was not quite three years old and I was so involved in her care. A hundred images came flooding back, in no particular order, fragments of carefree memories. And then I thought about the mothers in the maternity ward at Rothschild, those mothers who agreed to give up their babies so that they, too, would have a chance to survive.

What had we done to deserve this?

■ We had to explain to Bijou what was about to happen. She listened, her eyes wide open, her face serious, unquestioning. Maman, who had been so strong when my father was at Drancy, had changed. She seemed absent. Gone were the fits of anger, she just looked worn out, and her eyes were red every morning.

One day, Monsieur Dekeukelaere arrived, we embraced Bijou, our cheeks and our hands and our lips bathed in tears. And then she was gone, in a car that was waiting downstairs. It was toward the end of November 1942, the air was frigid, the avenue so sad it would make you weep. As for the apartment, it was like a battlefield following a defeat, with survivors wandering about aimlessly, surprised and ashamed to be alive, and not daring to speak to each other.

And my father continued to unveil his plan:

"We'll need to hide, too," he announced to us a few days later.

He draped his coat glistening with raindrops over a chair in the living room, barely lit by a miserable acetylene lamp.

"Damn cold, huh!"

Once his hands warmed up a bit, he spread out on the table three identity cards, perhaps looking a bit too new to be genuine, but nevertheless they seemed like the real thing.

"From now on, we are the Mosnier family, we've fled from Lorient, because, as you know, our house was bombed and we've moved to Paris."

"Why Lorient?"

"Because, my dear Colette, half of Lorient was destroyed by bombs, so no one will be able to verify the authenticity of our civil status. And here is what will feed us," he added, pulling wads of ration coupons out of his bag. "And don't worry," he said, reading my thoughts, "these are real coupons issued by the town hall. They are completely authentic."

"So we are Catholic," I said, in disbelief.

My father ducked his chin in agreement.

"Catholic and clandestine."

For a few moments, I wondered how I would manage at the hospital, where I'm known as Colette Brull, Jewish, and starred. Was I going to be able to go there under an assumed identity?

"We'll still have to wear the star for a few more days, for the time it will take to organize our move."

I said nothing, perplexed by the situation.

Some time later, we quietly left avenue Hoche for a tiny apartment in Neuilly, rue Jacques-Dulud. When I first saw it, carrying my fake refugee (but genuine clandestine) little suitcase, I was startled. Everything was old and dirty, with rancid odors that must been hanging around for years. Our hideout was a sort of excrescence on the ground floor of a building black with grime, two rooms with a kitchen and a basic bathroom. I took the tour with Papa.

In the cellar, he pulled back a grill that hid the entrance to a kind of subterranean passage.

"It looks like it goes to the sewers. If there's a problem, this will be our *escapatorium*," he said with a smile.

I barely smiled at his joke. I hadn't yet got used to his new face, emaciated but rejuvenated nonetheless, for the morning of our move he had shaved off his beard and mustache. I had almost forgotten he had a face like everyone else, a chin and a mouth. He looked completely different, like a man who was wily and determined, ruthless.

But exhausted and ill.

As for the star, he only wore it for a few days. One day, when we were going to take the métro, two teenage boys, seventeen or eighteen years old, barred the sidewalk, two pale weaklings, sure of their strength but royally stupid.

"Let's have a go at this old kike," the first one said to his buddy.

They egged each other on, bumping shoulders, sneering, and eying each other. I was close to fainting, my legs were beginning to buckle. I tried to hold back my father.

"No . . . no, leave it be."

As if in a dream (or a gangster movie, whichever), I saw him plant himself in front of the first kid and haul off a straight punch to the jaw that sent him rolling on the ground. The other one took two steps back, his shoulders drooping, already beaten. He started to beg, the coward.

"No, no, Monsieur, please . . ."

Meanwhile, the first one was having trouble getting up, moving slowly, blinking his eyes. They both ran off without looking back, as if they had seen the devil. My father had been in the trenches and knew hand-to-hand combat. How could he possibly be afraid of these two miserable idiots?

That evening he showed me his fist, which hurt. He had broken a bone in his finger.

▪ In our new life in Neuilly, we no longer risked these types of incidents. Although formally jobless and prone to frequent angina attacks, my father ran around Paris for mysterious meetings. It was pointless to try to find out whom he was seeing, he was as silent as the grave. Overnight, all our day-to-day problems were solved: Maman had all the ration coupons she needed and enough cash for the black market.

Where did this sudden prosperity come from when he no longer had a job?

He said nothing about it, but I was sure he was working for the Resistance. That would certainly have explained his reticence when I decided to continue working at Rothschild.

To each his own war, after all.

14

The Orphanage

It didn't take me long to get used to my new identity. Mademoiselle Colette Mosnier, refugee from Lorient, in the department of Morbihan, Brittany, rode the métro with everyone else to go to the hospital. From a distance, I could see poor Jews pushed to the end of the platform, waiting for a seat in the last carriage. I say "poor," because most of them had become truly impoverished, excluded from every job, every shop. While the wealthiest or the most resourceful might still show a bit of style, most were pale, their clothes patched; they slunk close to the walls, eyes downcast, on the lookout for identity checkpoints or for bullying, forever ready to apologize for anything.

All that made me terribly angry. Since I lived freely thanks to my father, since I could in principle escape their fate, I felt it was my duty to fight. What I didn't know, however, was the extent to which I would have the opportunity to do so.

Gougoutte knew about my new situation, and of course she immediately offered to help. Now in the mornings I no longer went directly to the cloakroom, but to her studio not far from Rothschild. There I left my clothes and false papers and slipped into my white coat with the star. I then crossed the hospital courtyard to begin my day. All of this was absolutely illegal and rather dangerous if I got caught (for Mademoiselle Damangout, too), but I didn't feel ready to give up my studies or my work.

Something about the Germans had changed. Their calm strength, cheerful confidence, that casual tourist look they sometimes displayed at the beginning had given way to worry. We also saw more wounded soldiers on convalescence, decorated men old before their time, who we supposed were survivors of the eastern front.

The winds had shifted: they had lost at Stalingrad, and their propaganda couldn't alter that fact. On the pediments of public buildings, they flew their disgusting flags at half-mast. But most of all, you could read the change on their faces.

We secretly watched them, with fierce satisfaction. One evening in the lab, we uncorked a bottle.

"Long live Stalin!" exclaimed an intern, so loudly that we all turned toward the door.

"Let's not exaggerate."

"I'm not exaggerating. Without him, no one would have stopped Hitler."

"Maybe, but if you keep on braying like that, we're the ones who will be stopped."

Gougoutte raised her glass. "To the end of the war!"

None of us dared speak of victory yet, but all of us thought about it. We drank, our eyes glowing, and the conversation turned to how long the war would last, to what we would do after, to what the Americans might do now that they had landed in North Africa.

A glimmer of light had appeared in the shadows.

■ Nearly every day, I ran into Danielle. It was like seeing my little Bijou again; I missed her so horribly much now that she was in exile. We did get news from Monsieur Dekeukelaere. Bijou had safely arrived in Belgium, everything was going well, but I tried not to think about it too much. It was just too sad.

Danielle must also have been suffering from not seeing her parents, but she said nothing about it. As soon as she saw me, she'd come running into my arms. Every day she learned new words, and I took time to listen to her tell me the little things she had seen, what the policeman at the entrance had said to her, the piece of cake she'd been given, the dream or nightmare of the previous night, the big discoveries she'd made in the ward or at a turn in the path.

I no longer asked questions about her, we had so many reasons to worry, why add another? If she was still here, it was because they had not found a way to get her out. Whatever happened, we believed that the hospital would always be a refuge.

And yet the warning signs were multiplying.

Very early one morning in February 1943, when I had just arrived at the general medicine pavilion and was there on my own, the door burst open and a nurse rushed in. She seemed panic-stricken: a doctor was wanted on the phone.

"I answered that there wasn't one, but the caller insisted. It seems serious. I couldn't understand what was happening."

I frowned. On the other end of the line, a woman in charge at the Rothschild Orphanage explained to me, breathlessly, that one or several of the children were unwell, that they were having fits of hysterics, and that they absolutely needed a doctor. I asked her for some details, to no avail. She seemed half crazy to me, or like someone calling from a burning building.

"Come quickly," she said before hanging up.

Without bothering to slip on a coat or let anyone know, I grabbed some bottles of a sedative syrup and ran out past the policemen's post, where they waved at me unaware of what was going on. The orphanage was on rue Lamblardie, a five-minute walk from the hospital. About one hundred children lived there, most of whose parents had been deported.

Proof, if any was needed, of the cynicism of the Nazis, who continued to claim not *to want to separate families.*

I was surprised to see a police van parked in front of the old orphanage building. Outside, everything seemed calm, but inside, it was a real nightmare. For a long time after, I refused to think about that moment, those horrible moments. A whole lifetime has not been long enough to find the right words. I froze like a pillar of salt. The whole building was filled with screams, screaming such as I'd never heard—screams of absolute, immeasurable terror. For a moment, I was unable to move, stupefied, my mouth hanging open, incapable of thinking or acting, my bottles in hand. Someone was talking to me, but I couldn't hear anything.

Gradually the scene emerged from the fog, as if I needed time to transform into thoughts what my eyes were seeing. A shadow was fleeing down the stairs, a kid of ten, perhaps, barefoot and in pajamas. A policeman was chasing him down the steps, clumsily, treading heavily. The thud of his hobnailed soles shook the walls, while the weapon on his back swung back and forth with every step, banging against them.

In the large dormitory, the sheets had been thrown on the floor.

And everywhere there were children running around and screaming.

The monitors were huddled in a corner, pale, as if anesthetized. On their faces, I saw the same despair, the horror of knowing they should do something, but that there was nothing they could do. Next to them, a cop had a list in his hands, trying to give some semblance of order to this hellish scene. Another cop kept a group of children backed up against a wall, as if they were criminals. Most were in their pajamas, sobbing, kids ten years old, some younger, who had no idea what was happening, and who were calling out for their mothers.

I went over and gave them a little water and some medicine to calm them down. Someone then called me down to the basement, to the cellar where the orphan hunt was in full swing. It was dark and full of old furniture and battered boxes that the children were trying to hide behind.

"There!" trumpeted a policeman, calling to me, as if he expected me to help him.

Despite the cold, his dirt-smudged forehead was dripping with sweat, his cap pushed back on his head. A shadow slipped toward the exit, collided with a monitor, turned back toward the cellar where it disappeared once more.

I went back upstairs, in a daze.

Little by little, the screaming stopped. I still had the syrup in my hands, and we tried to calm the children, who were quivering like caged birds.

The policeman in charge counted and recounted, checking the names, crossing some off, his face impassive. What was he feeling? Surely he had kids of his own, maybe kids the same age. How could he for one moment believe that these children *had* to be arrested, that it was really necessary to send them God knows where in sealed freight cars? Because the cops, they *knew*, just like we knew. Maybe they didn't know about Auschwitz, but they knew about the wagons, they knew it wasn't good.

So what was he thinking, this policeman with his list?

"There's one missing. Yes, a female," he said after a moment. "Hedwige Plaut. She's seven. Has anyone seen her?"

He looked first at his men and then at the orphanage directors, who stood stock still. He pursed his lips and stuck his nose back into his list. He counted and recounted.

"She must be hiding somewhere," he murmured, as if talking to himself.

The search turned up nothing. The dormitory seemed dead, the cellar deserted. On his orders, the monitors gathered up the belongings—

toys, underwear, pictures, all those little childish possessions that would wind up torn to pieces and tossed to the winds. They lined up the orphans, some of them still sobbing, hiccupping great tears, and then they departed. The silence rang with the drumming of the policemen's hobnailed shoes, the creaking of the leather straps on their equipment, the clanging of the steel of their weapons. Doors slammed shut and the truck labored off, wheezing.

An immense silence now fell on the orphanage. It seemed to me that the roundup had lasted for hours, but it had only been ten minutes since I had arrived. Some of the personnel were crying; I think the director was too. And there I was with my stupid medicine bottles in my hands. And we stood there, our arms dangling, as if we all had been punched silly. Knocked out, but still standing.

■ When my workday ended, I slowly walked to the métro, feeling as though I had emerged from hell. I didn't get it. How could anyone give orders, send cops, lose time and money, waste all that energy, stage this formidable exercise, just to go after a few defenseless children?

I recounted what I had seen, we ate, and then I went to study. A little later, my father knocked at my door:

"I know what you're feeling," he said to me. "But this proves one thing. Rothschild is becoming dangerous. You should stop going there."

I kept my nose stuck in my anatomy book.

"You'll finish your studies after the war is over."

"When?!"

"It won't last forever. Stalin has begun his offensive in Russia. The Allies are going to land in France. The war will not last forever, Colette. Believe me."

I went back to my reading, twiddling my pencil with my right hand.

"They need me there."

"Of course they do. But you run the risk of being arrested if you continue to go there without the star. And what will you have gained if you get caught? If you really want to do something, you know you can do it with me."

I didn't answer.

Behind the blacked-out windows, the city was silent, and so was our building. And in this silence, I could still hear the children screaming, the tromping of the police. Of course my father was right. Just taking the métro was enormously dangerous. Checks were performed all the time: riders were stopped, their papers and belongings inspected, always in search of the same things—black market goods, leaflets, weapons, anything that could send the culprit to prison, or worse.

And the Jew in hiding was always the catch of choice, the coveted prize.

My eyes were still fixed on the illustrated plates of muscles and nerves. My father sighed.

"As you wish. Don't stay up too late," he said, gently closing the door behind him.

Silence once more.

Later, I got into bed but couldn't fall asleep. I could still hear the screams of the children.

◾ On that day, some fifteen or so innocent Jewish children were sent to their deaths, none of them French. The orphanage closed soon after, and the remaining children were evacuated.*

---

*The remaining children were placed in UGIF homes or smuggled out through the hospital's underground network. In March 1943, the orphanage was reopened as a hospice for elderly prisoners from Drancy. Immediately after the war, it became an orphanage once again and served as an infant and maternity center for displaced Jewish women and children.

Then I learned something else. It seemed there had been one survivor. One child saved from Rothschild.

It was whispered that it was a little girl who had hidden under the sheets while the others panicked and tried to flee, that they found her motionless in her bed, bathed in tears, but lying as still as death. They said she had not spoken a word since they found her.

It also appeared that she had been surreptitiously whisked away.

For years I have been haunted by the memory of that roundup. I would hear the howls of the children and see the policemen with their weapons. Torn between the horror of these memories and the remorse I felt for being powerless to act, I preferred silence. Even my own children were barely aware of what I had lived through. Then, much later in life, I began to speak up.

One day, in the late 1990s, I participated in a memorial gathering at the hospital and spoke to the audience about the roundup at the orphanage. At the exit, a woman came up to me and introduced herself; she was around sixty years old.

"I am Hedwige Plaut," she said. "I was the little girl under the covers."

I stared at her, completely dumbfounded.

Half a century had passed. She was now a mature woman, with a serious expression, perhaps a little too serious, as if she were locked from the inside, even after all these years. She told me her story. The orphanage was not the peaceful haven we imagined it to be. The children were starving, they were cold and afraid all the time. Despite all efforts made by the personnel, the youngest ones' food was often stolen. She also remembered Christmas 1942 and the toy she was given then.

But most of all, she remembered the roundup.

"When the police arrived, I hid under the sheets and didn't move. I heard everything going on around me, but I didn't budge, it was like I was dead. After, I didn't speak about it for years. I wanted to forget."

It was her husband's love that finally drew her out of her silence. She had been the only survivor; her name had mysteriously disappeared from the list of children to be deported.

She was then taken in charge by an underground network—OSE, Oeuvre de secours aux enfants, a Jewish children's aid organization that had entered into resistance. With a group of around thirty children, who were being hunted as she was, she set out on a long journey, a hellish odyssey that finally led them to the Swiss frontier. The journey was made day and night, by train, by truck, even on foot. In the brutal last hours they had to cross streams, traverse ravines.

"Some of us disappeared," Hedwige recounted. "Of the twenty-nine who set out, half didn't make it there."

Subsequently she was adopted by a Swiss family and later reunited with her mother, who had also escaped the disaster. I felt that she was still suffering, but she had lived and she had loved. She had escaped the fate that had been planned for her and had lived out her own destiny—despite the heartbreak, despite everything.

That was our greatest victory.

The orphanage roundup was a warning. The Nazis would fill their trains no matter what. Every day, or so it seemed, I saw people stopped and searched in the métro. And the Germans no longer even pretended to appear *correct*, as they had in 1940. For a while now, they had been accompanied by zealous henchmen, Darnand's militia* in black

---

*Joseph Darnand, Vichy collaborator and founder of the Milice, a paramilitary militia supported by the Nazi government in Paris. Sentenced to death and executed October 19, 1945.

uniforms or members of Doriot's PPF,* imbeciles who were convinced of a German victory, or poor creatures drawn in by the prospect of a reward.

I thought about it every day when I got to the hospital.

Danielle was no longer the scared child that we knew at the beginning, but the hospital's child who knew its hidden corners better than I did. I was always so pleased to see her, hold her in my arms, feel her curls on my cheeks. She was speaking better and better although she was only three, and when there was time, we had long conversations, like those, I'm sure, between a mother and child. And I wasn't the only one enchanted by her little words and her peals of laughter.

Her stay at Rothschild got longer, but I continued to tell myself that someone was going to find a solution for her. For some time now, I had known this was possible.

Yes, there was an escape network for children here. Claire Heyman ran it and she asked me to be a part of it.

*Jacques Doriot, founder of the ultra-nationalist PPF, Parti Populaire français, in 1936. Collaborator who fought with the Germans on the Eastern Front. Killed in 1945 when his car was strafed by Allied fighter planes.

15

Escapes

■ For months, I had been dying to act. I have to say that my father had taught me well. Like him, I was revolted by the German occupation and outraged by the attitude of Pétain and his government.

On November 11, 1940, I was among the few thousand high school and university students who came to lay wreaths at the Tomb of the Unknown Soldier. The Germans dispersed the demonstrators with the butts of their rifles and warning shots fired into the air, but I had missed all that: I got there late.

Since that moment my determination had just grown stronger. The anti-Jewish measures, especially the brutal acts and horrors that I had witnessed myself, kindled in me an irrepressible desire for revenge. I could not tolerate the abusive treatment of children and the elderly.

I tried not to show my feelings too openly, especially now that I was in hiding, but I guess they were pretty clear nonetheless. To tell the truth, I was so angry I felt I was capable of just about anything.

One day, a classmate quietly came to sound me out, carefully choosing his words.

"You know, Colette, I have some friends . . . There are some papers to distribute."

I accepted right away, and I didn't care for a moment what it was that had to be distributed. Communist tracts, Gaullist tracts, anything, it was all the same to me as long as it was anti-German.

"OK," I told him. "What must I do?"

"I'll let you know," he answered before we separated. But he never did contact me.

Father Kenneth, the Irish priest from avenue Hoche, proved to be more serious.

After he arranged for Maurice's escape, we got along well. He told me his curious life story. Before he became a priest, he lived in grand style in czarist Russia. But in 1917, his fiancée was killed and he had to flee a country in flames. Finding refuge in a Benedictine order, he eventually became a priest.

In the course of our conversations, he let me know that he was involved in underground activities; that's how he knew smugglers at the line of demarcation . . . But there was more than that . . . At times he worked for a certain organization . . . And as he became more sure of me, he told me that for a long time he had been in British Intelligence and was recently reactivated.

One day, he asked to speak to me in private.

"Colette, I'm at a bit of a loss. I have a lad who is injured. Could you take a look at him?"

An injured lad. Obviously, this was connected to his espionage activities, but that was not what was bothering me the most.

"I'm only an intern. It's not serious, is it?"

"Don't worry. It's only a minor wound. Can you?"

"Of course I can!"

A short time later, we left avenue Hoche on foot (this was before my father's unexpected release), me with my little kit of bandages and disinfectant—highly suspect items if misfortune struck and we were searched in the métro. I unstitched the star on my coat and followed Father Kenneth. He walked at a good clip, clearly above suspicion, while I felt I was being stared at by everyone on the street, me and my first aid kit.

My heart was pounding so fast I could feel it in my throat, choking me.

After a good hour's walk, we arrived at the Gare Saint-Lazare, on the other side of the train tracks. I tried not to look at the street names or numbers. To know nothing (or as little as possible), that was the surest way not to talk if beaten or tortured, because that was really what we were risking.

The priest discreetly glanced about the street before pushing open the door of an apartment building. I followed him up to the top floor, where the *lad* in question, wearing a grayish shirt and blue trousers, was alone in a garret. He was about my age and very calmly he showed me his hands, which were both badly burned. I dressed his wounds without us exchanging a word. Then I realized he didn't understand a single word of French.

He was a downed British aviator, and God knows by what miracle he had fallen into Father Kenneth's hands. Many years later I found out—you really don't know much in a war—that his church on avenue Hoche was one of the addresses given to Allied airmen if they were shot down in the Paris region. Still, even knowing that, his presence there was astonishing: how had this aviator been able to get across an occupied city where he didn't speak the language, with his hands burned and this tattered uniform on his back?

Subsequently, I treated at least one other wounded airman. Father Kenneth took me under his wing, and I helped him produce false baptismal certificates as well as counterfeit Irish citizenship papers for people whose identity I preferred not to know.

At that time, we were living on avenue Hoche. While Father Kenneth and I worked, Maurice and Bijou were asked to stay in their rooms. We spent long hours at the table in the living room making the counterfeit documents look as authentic as possible.

And they all went to his network.

I assume he would have entrusted me with other jobs, but we moved to Neuilly and, more important, from then on I devoted myself entirely to the hospital, where Claire Heyman regularly called on me.

■ Now it was no longer just a matter of prolonging hospital stays or fiddling with diagnoses; now it was about rescuing children.

This all began sometime after the Vélodrome d'hiver roundup, when our pavilions were beginning to be jammed with sick people, young and old. One day, I heard a voice call out to me as I was crossing between two pavilions.

It was Claire Heyman.

"Colette, I need to talk to you," she said to me.

She quickly glanced around before continuing the conversation in a perfectly ordinary tone of voice.

"I have a job for you. We have to get some children out. Can you do that?"

Get some children out? It was very clear what she meant: smuggle them out.

For a few seconds, I was jolted by this confirmation that, yes, she was the one running the network.

Actually I was not so surprised. As Rothschild's social worker, Claire Heyman knew everything about the sick children. If certain family members were still at liberty, she could approach them about taking them in. And if there was no family, she had contacts in every orphanage, every charitable organization, secular or religious, every possible port in the storm.

And she was certainly one of the best placed people to recruit accomplices from within the hospital, as she was doing with me.

It was extremely risky, mad even. For these kids belonged to the Nazi administration; they were prisoners, they were on file. I assumed that before she organized their escapes, she had to erase their names from the registers in such a way as to make it appear that they had never been *officially admitted.* Erase any and all administrative trace. I realized, too, that she must be the one who organized the disappearances of newborns in the maternity wing.

And all this was being done from inside an annex of Drancy, the antechamber to deportation. One of the most tightly surveilled places in France. Any prison director is aware that prisoners most often try to escape from the infirmary or the hospital. That's the case in every country and in every jail in the world. Feign an illness, report sick, and then use the hospital to make a run for it.

These thoughts were all running through my mind as I looked at her. From her appearance, she looked completely above suspicion, a young woman calm and unremarkable, serious and discreet. But in fact she was a war commander, ready to take any risk for the children.

I accepted on the spot.

"When? What do I have to do?"

She smiled at me, her eyes resting briefly on my star, on the white coat, and then on the paths around us.

"Come back tonight. Without the star. I'll wait for you in my office and I'll tell you what to do."

The day unfolded without incident. I went home to tell my parents I'd be late, and in the evening when I returned, the hospital was quietly ensconced in the dark of night. The grounds were empty, gloomy, only a few lights shone in the windows of some pavilions. From his sentry box, the policeman on duty, bored stiff, waved absently to me. I could only see part of his face, lit by a single bulb. He must have thought that I was taking the night shift.

But once I passed the entrance, I headed not for my usual pavilion, but for the one where Claire Heyman had her office. The place was deserted, and my footsteps echoed in the empty corridor. She closed the door behind us after a brief look around.

"We have a little time," she said, sitting down. "You'll be taking two children, but I'll introduce them to you later. I hope you have good shoes?"

"They're OK," I replied, a bit surprised. "Why?"

"Because you can't take the métro. You'll have to walk. You have to go to the fifteenth arrondissement, rue d'Alleray, do you know where that is?"

I wasn't expecting that, but these kids didn't have papers so of course there was no question of us taking the métro; identity checks made it too dangerous. Claire showed me the route on a map: go down toward the Seine, up on the other side to place Denfert-Rochereau, then walk to the fifteenth. More than eight kilometers.

In other words, about a two-hour walk with two kids in tow.

"Walk normally and don't look around all the time," she said, as she led me to a small room farther down, where two children I had never seen before were waiting (later on, I guessed they had come from the orphanage).

The older one, the little girl, was maybe six years old. She must have been more or less expecting me because she didn't seem surprised. She was pale, probably because it was late in the evening, but also because she was nervous. Her brother, who was not yet three, barely noticed us coming in.

"So off we go, all three of us?" I said to the little girl, with a tight smile that I hoped was reassuring.

Truth be told, I was not so reassured myself. To cross the city with these two kids in complete illegality, and with all I was risking . . .

The little girl nodded without saying a word, her eyes filled with a mix of terror and confidence that broke my heart.

"Don't worry," Claire Heyman told her tenderly. "I've explained to you that the lady who is taking you is very kind, everything will be fine. You'll be brave, won't you?"

Another nod.

We left the building, and I remember how tiny the boy's steps were. He couldn't walk very fast, so I stopped to pick him up, a little surprised to find how heavy he was. Then the four of us walked to the morgue, beside the hospital wall. Opening onto rue Santerre was a door that wasn't guarded.

We moved forward cautiously in the dark. I was already out of breath, my arms straining from the boy's weight. And I'd have to walk for two hours like this! Usually, the morgue door was locked, but not that evening, as I had anticipated. On the other side, a dark chasm: rue Santerre, completely empty. Claire quietly opened the door and carefully surveyed the street, a quick precaution. Clearly she wasn't doing this for the first time.

Who else besides me was smuggling children out?

"And don't forget," she said, while signaling me that the road was clear. "Rue d'Alleray. You can't miss it. It's a big entrance with a cross above it, you'll remember that? Just ring, they'll be waiting for you. No need for names; they know what's going on."

We looked at each other, I took a deep breath and began to walk.

Claire warned me that, apart from the possible checkpoints we might run into, the most dangerous moment was going to be at the very beginning, rue Santerre: I could encounter someone from the hospital—doctor, patient, policeman, anyone who might not look kindly on rescuing children. A young intern in her twenties suddenly relieved of her yellow star, out in the night with two children who had no papers . . . My case would not have been difficult to figure out.

So I started to breathe normally again only as I got closer to place de la Nation, before heading down toward the Seine. *Breathe* being a bit of an exaggeration because after a few minutes I was sweating and out of breath. The little boy was awfully heavy; I felt I was carrying a lump of lead. Like some children, he didn't think to hang on to my neck and was constantly slipping down on my hips. I had to boost him up every five hundred meters with a thrust of my hip just to reposition him. This quickly became torture. Fortunately, the little girl was a good walker, trotting at my side in the dark, not looking around, not saying a word. I felt her small hand gripping mine, as if I were her buoy in a sea of uncertainty.

We crossed the Seine around the Gare d'Austerlitz. Paris was sleeping under a mantle of darkness and silence, passersby were few and automobiles even fewer. An hour later, I was still walking, exhausted, my elbow in agony. There was no way in the world that I would stop for more than a minute. That could get me noticed, and I didn't want that at any cost. In my head, I was a young woman taking her niece and nephew back to their home, which was why I was carrying neither papers nor bags.

I suppose that this story would have been ridiculed had we been stopped, but fortunately that did not happen. After an eternity, I reached Montparnasse. I stopped a time or two to catch my breath, but mostly to get my blood circulating in my aching arm. How the devil could this pint-size little guy be so heavy? Luckily, the two kids said not a word and didn't complain. They reminded me of small, hunted animals who freeze in place and stay silent to survive.

Rue d'Alleray, at last.

Just a few more steps to the address Claire had given me, a rather imposing stone porch, above which rose a cross, like she had said. It was obviously a religious institution, a monastery or convent. After I rang, I didn't have long to wait. A peephole opened, then the door, with a heavy creak. Two hands emerged from the shadows, I set the boy down, my lower back and arms on fire, and gently pushed the little girl forward.

She looked at me one last time, her eyes full of questions.

"You're here," I said to her. "Go on, this is it."

She still hesitated so I nudged her forward again. I added, rather stupidly:

"I have the children."

No one bothered to reply.

The door closed again slowly, and the two children were swallowed up in the darkness, leaving no trace behind. Undoubtedly they would not be staying there long. There would be other journeys in the night, other silences, other hands held out to them, of which I would know nothing. But the main thing was this: they were now safe, far from Drancy and the Bourget railway station.

I took a few steps to regain my breath, empty and exhausted, soaked in sweat, feeling like my arm had been jammed under a barrel. It was a long way home and I had to hurry to make the curfew.

■ I gave my report to Claire Heyman. She thanked me and smiled, and we left it there.

The fear came later, fueled by all those things you think of afterward that could have gone wrong: fear of being stopped, of going to the wrong address, fear that the children would not cooperate, that they would make a scene in the middle of the street. After all, I didn't know them, and they may not have understood where they were going.

But none of that happened, so . . .

More than forty years after the war, I took part in a public meeting about the Rothschild Hospital, at which time I described that first rescue. Afterward, a woman came up to me, petite, about sixty, with an anxious look on her face that was intensified by the circles of kohl around her eyes.

Her voice was unsteady as she told me her story.

In 1942, she was eight years old, and her brother a little more than three. Their father had been arrested a year earlier, and the Vélodrome d'hiver roundup had made it their turn. At that time, she had scabies.

"Stick close to your sister," their mother ordered the little boy. Then to the little girl, "If he does that, he'll catch it, too, and they'll take you both to the infirmary."

Good idea: by touching and rubbing against each other, both brother and sister were evacuated from the Vél d'hiv to Rothschild. Their mother, who had suffered a bad fall and hurt her back, went with them.

One day, their mother was gone from the hospital, and when the little boy realized it, he had a nervous breakdown. He ran around the grounds, calling for his mother. They had to pull him off a tree he was gripping onto, screaming his head off; he even fell ill with a violent depression. As a result, the two children stayed at the hospital for several months. The woman had no particular memory of it, apart from the barbed wire around the pavilions. The two became absolutely inseparable, for the little girl had received one last assignment from her mother before she disappeared:

"Whatever happens, look after your brother, stay with him."

She had obeyed her, throughout the war and even after.

According to this woman, Aunt Claire—that's what she called her—*got them out*. When and how, she could not recall. All she remembered was a journey, by bus or truck, where they were hidden under blankets. They were taken to a chateau, the name of which she never knew. Someone unstitched their stars and they were given new names that were less obvious.

"You are now Durand," they told her. "Durand and nothing else, do you understand?"

At the end of the war, she found refuge at the Rothschild Orphanage, without ever being separated from her brother. Aunt Claire came to see them regularly, like a substitute mother. They always stayed in touch, right to the end. One day, while chatting with them, she confided that she had indeed organized the escapes. And that's all she said.

On reflection, she was perhaps the only person to whom Claire Heyman ever clearly admitted her true role.

I quickly imagined that the two children I had saved under Claire's direction were this woman and her brother, but she was persuaded otherwise. In her memory, the escape took place at night, certainly, but in a bus or truck and under a blanket. The trek across Paris meant nothing to her. And I also thought to myself that *my* little girl and her brother were younger than this woman and her brother would have been at the time.

So what became of the two children I smuggled out that evening? Was it this woman and her brother? Or others? I'll never know, but it doesn't really matter. Nothing mattered, except saving children.

In addition to those two, I remember saving at least two others, always the same way: leaving by the morgue door, at night, without the star. After all these years my memories are somewhat vague. Everything was done in secret, in silence, always trying to know as little as possible, as I had done with the wounded airmen. Once the war was over, I did everything I could to forget what I had lived through. The memories were too painful.

Inevitably, I almost ended up forgetting for good.

How many children were saved, nobody knows. How could you count them, on which registers would their names have been entered? When I met this woman who had been saved by Claire Heyman, she told me a disturbing fact: after the war, she had encountered enormous difficulty obtaining identification papers. There was no trace of her movements or even of her existence, anywhere, and least of all, at the hospital. Administratively, she no longer existed.

This confirmed my intuition, that these children had been saved not only physically, but also *administratively*, like all the newborns in the maternity department who had been declared stillborn. This epidemic had camouflaged a rescue network. For a long while, I believed that we saved maybe twenty or thirty children. I now believe that number is far higher.

But how many in all?

Several dozen, several hundred? No one will ever know. Only Claire Heyman could have told us, but she died and left no testimony.

I don't know if we should regret this or not.

My real regret, my eternal regret, is for something else.

16

Danielle

The day I would never forget began like every other day. I must have gotten dressed and had my ersatz coffee. My father, as he did every day, must have nagged me about the dangers of continuing to go to the hospital with false papers. I took the métro nonetheless and stopped by Gougoutte's to change into my white coat with its star—just like every other day. Nothing out of the ordinary.

From their loge at the entrance, the policemen waved at me. From habit, we wound up getting to know each other, sort of like colleagues. Certainly they were a different type of colleague because their presence reminded us that the hospital was a prison, but sometimes we wound up forgetting that too. Some of them may have come here reluctantly, they may have even been quiet resisters, like the policemen who warned Jews they were about to be arrested. If you think about it, they were even our accomplices to some extent, for never once had there been a denunciation when a child disappeared or when a stay was prolonged. And the cops had the best seats in the house; from there any suspicious mind would certainly have suspected such things.

Like most of us, they had fallen for Danielle's charm. Like me, some of them spent a little of their time with her, playing with her, giving her little gifts. How could they not?

On that day, I must have crossed paths with them, her and her sister. She must have said hello in her clear voice, put her tiny arms around my neck; I must have asked her how she was feeling and what she was going to do that day.

"I have to leave now and go to work, I'm sure we'll see each other later."

The day went by, unremarkably, no doubt, while around me, the stage was set, like the backdrop of a tragedy whose characters inexorably advance toward their destiny. And no one can do anything about it.

In every human group, there are always men who are more servile and cowardly than others, or who are devoid of scruples. You couldn't tell it by his face. He was still a young man, maybe in his thirties, but he carried himself like a man who was already well established, serious, calm, sure of himself, who knew what he was doing and why. We saw him arrive, dressed in his dark suit, anonymous, a bureaucrat like any other. It didn't seem to me that I'd met him before.

"I am Doctor B. from the infirmary at Drancy," he announced to the head of general medicine, a former hospital doctor.

The news spread through the hospital in a flash. So Drancy, in other words, the Germans, had decided on an inspection. When they were unsuccessful in filling up their next train, they sent in their henchmen. This time, it was worse: they sent in a doctor, not a soldier or a policeman. This time, we would not be able to cheat.

He began his inspection. Gougoutte followed him, her face outwardly passive, but she must have been feeling scared. From where I was, I could see him walking from bed to bed, unhurriedly asking questions, examining patients without even consulting their temperature charts, X-rays, or medical files.

Time seemed suspended, each of us attending to our little jobs absentmindedly, like extras in a movie. We all eyed the little group as discreetly as possible. And we exchanged looks that seemed to say, "Let's hope it all goes well. Let's hope he's not as hard as he looks." No one knew this Doctor B., and we tried to reassure ourselves. After all, he couldn't be as crazy as Dannecker, the Nazi who struck patients and threatened Leibovici with his pistol.

No, it couldn't be as terrible as that.

Maybe he even knew that children were being rescued, and more or less looked the other way.

After he finished in our department, he headed for another pavilion. At that time of day, many of the patients were usually outside for the fresh air, especially since spring had gently arrived. However, on that day there weren't many because we had sent out the message to act *as sick as possible.*

Was this why B. caught sight of Danielle? I don't know. In any case, he came across her playing quietly on the grounds.

"So, who are these kids?"

Displeased, he challenged Gougoutte.

"They are little girls. They're sick. Probably a primary infection . . ."

B. gave her a black look.

"They don't look sick. A primary infection?"

"I mean . . . Yes. The older girl is always getting sore throats. Actually, the other one too. They're rather frail. They're better off here than at Drancy."

He shrugged his shoulders.

"These kids are perfectly healthy. Send them back to Drancy immediately."

"But . . . There's a risk. They are frail. . . ."

Interminable silence. He looked at Gougoutte carefully, expressionless. Then he looked back at Danielle, but it was not the way you look at a child, rather it was the way you look at something dangerous or dirty. At best Danielle was just a name on a list for him, but she didn't count as a child.

I kept an eye on him too. What was he thinking at that moment? He was a doctor in the public hospitals, a good position at his age. He had sought the job at the infirmary at Drancy. He knew the conditions the detainees lived in, as well as the conditions of the departures. Surely he couldn't believe any more than we did about some type of work in the East. He knew that no one ever heard from detainees once they had been deported. He knew that some prisoners preferred to take their own lives rather than be put on the trains.

He knew.

He could have served in any number of hospitals or had a practice in the city, done a thousand other things in a thousand other places. But no, he was here, a meticulous Nazi henchman, as if it mattered to him that this little girl get on the train with her parents. As if he couldn't close his eyes just this once and show a little humanity.

A ridiculously meticulous idiot.

I detested him already. A wave of hatred came over me, flushing my cheeks and leaving me trembling. *Go away! Just go away! Leave them alone, you bastard!*

Danielle and Céline had stopped playing, they were looking at him, without fear, but on their guard just the same.

"Send them back to Drancy. They have no business being here."

He turned away to continue his visit. Case closed. But not for Gougoutte, who continued to trot at his side, ignoring the risks she was taking.

"But, Doctor, you know very well. We can't send them back to Drancy, they're fine here."

"They aren't sick. There's no reason to keep them here."

"In Drancy, they'll get sick again. They may get tuberculosis."

He kept walking, seemingly annoyed.

"There are dozens of children in Drancy. They do just fine."

"If we send them back, they'll be deported. And their parents too. It's . . ."

This time he stopped cold and stared at Gougoutte.

"What is your name?"

She gave her name and title, turning red. She had probably never dared speak to a superior like that.

"You are a head nurse, Mademoiselle. Is that correct?" he said, looking down at her, scornfully.

She nodded her head and swallowed hard.

"Then stick to your job. I understand that you get attached to your patients, but they do not belong to you. Do you follow me?"

"Of course, doctor, but they are . . ."

"These Jews are internees at Drancy. That means they have been arrested and belong to the camp authorities, and so they belong to the Germans. You know what that means?"

Gougoutte nodded her head, livid with impotence and rage. At that moment, I pitied her but I also wanted to take her place so I could spit in this bastard's face, tell him to get the hell out, leave us alone, and let the children be. I knew she felt the same. Like her, I was burning inside from this shame of feeling enslaved, condemned to kowtow to this piece of filth.

"That means," continued B. in a soft voice, "that I have to report back to the Germans. And you know what that means, don't you? So none of that with me, Mademoiselle. This is a hospital, not a boarding school. I hope you will manage to remember this."

He then continued walking toward another pavilion, and Gougoutte followed on his heels. This time he came to a dead stop and swung around to face her.

"Did you not understand?"

"Yes, but I . . ."

"You should already be back in your department, taking care of the transfer. And now, Mademoiselle, I have some good advice for you: do not interfere with doctors and see to it that I never hear about you again."

■ B. spent as much time as he needed at the hospital, indifferent and merciless. No one dared address him again about the little girls. What good would it have done? Gougoutte had already gone as far as one could go.

That afternoon, no one worked much. The two little girls were whisked off to a room, as if they had to be protected from something. I went to see Danielle and told her that perhaps things would work out, that up to that point things had always worked out. But I had a hard time believing that myself.

"We're going back to see Maman, right?"

She looked at me with a new gleam in her eyes, of hope, maybe. But maybe it was also fear. The world around her had a crack in it. "It's not for certain. For the moment, you're still here."

With these words, I felt tears in my eyes and turned my head. I said it, but I didn't believe it. It was the bitter taste of defeat.

"The man said I was supposed to go back to Drancy. Céline said we are going back to Drancy, too."

"I don't know."

Her eyes were now filled with the same fear and sadness as when she had arrived the year before. Why had we done nothing? Why was she still here?

"I'll come back," I said to her before leaving the room.

The day was ending mildly with a springtime sun that grazed the lawn, a soft sky laden with puffy clouds, air that was almost still. Nothing had changed and yet the staging now seemed mortally sad: with all these walls, all these useless doors, it was an absurd and hopeless place. We had convinced ourselves that we were really protecting them, Danielle and her sister, that the hospital was truly their refuge; we had chosen to forget about the barbed wire and the convoys making their way to Germany. In one blow, reality returned, terrible and brutal, with no way out. Like the resurgence of a long-forgotten nightmare, unchanged, that annihilates you in an instant.

Claire Heyman surely had tried to smuggle the girls out, but it had not been possible; now it was too late. There would have been reprisals, the network would have been compromised, as well as all the patients.

We waited a bit, the time it took B. to finally leave the hospital, but not without leaving strict orders.

Gougoutte heard us go over the incident, propose I don't know how many idiotic solutions, become indignant, call B. every name in the book, but she barely listened, the light had gone out of her eyes.

I finished my day in a blur, swinging between rage and despondency. I barely noticed the patients in front of me. I just couldn't conceive that Danielle was really being ripped from me, that this was all true, that she was really leaving for Drancy and that she would really be put on a train. Who could do this sort of thing?

Toward the end of the afternoon, I heard footsteps approaching, big hobnailed shoes that startled me.

"Mademoiselle Brull?"

I turned around. It was one of the policemen on duty, looking so distraught that for a moment I thought that he had come to announce yet another catastrophe.

"What is it?"

"You know, about the little girl?"

I nodded, suddenly remembering that I had sometimes seen him with Danielle. He was undoubtedly a man with his own family, maybe even had his own little girl who looked like Danielle. I immediately forgot his uniform. He was just a worried father, a human being with feelings, who must have played with her, laughed with her, maybe lifted her into his arms.

He was like me. He couldn't understand it, he didn't accept it. He looked around briefly before continuing:

"B." (he almost whispered his name) "has put the girls on the lists. There's nothing me and my men can do now."

My head was spinning. I didn't understand what he wanted from me. I knew very well they couldn't do anything. So what did he mean?

"But we aren't obligated to send them back today," he said, in the same whisper. "We have to order a truck, all that stuff. We can wait . . ."

"How long?"

My heart started thumping with hope. He understood and shook his head sadly. "That's not what I meant, doctor. Only until tomorrow. To-morrow morning the truck will be here. Then we'll have to . . ."

Then he fell silent, his tearful words stuck in his throat. In an instant I felt terribly close to him. We shared the same powerlessness. And already the same remorse.

"But we have to do something," he continued. "We can't let them leave."

"I know we can't. But what can we do?"

He looked at me, searching for the right words, glancing furtively around the hospital grounds. The day hesitated to come to an end; in the distance, the horizon was turning a dark blue.

"I don't know," he repeated, obstinately. "With my men, we managed to put things off till tomorrow morning. That leaves you tonight. . . ."

His faded blue eyes met mine, the eyes of a man in his prime but tired, his eyelids drooping. A policeman used to petty crimes, swindlers, thieves, maybe even killers, he was anything but naïve. Of course he had noticed children disappearing, those little patients who arrived but never went back to Drancy.

But my God, what was he implying? That we should smuggle them out? That they wouldn't say anything? My head was buzzing with ideas. No, it was impossible. They, too, would immediately pay the price, be fired at best, imprisoned perhaps. What did he mean?

Our eyes met once more, then he gently shook my hand and went back to his loge, leaving me alone and confused. Maybe there was a small hope, like a glimmer of red in the embers of a fire that the slightest puff of air could either rekindle or extinguish forever.

"So, we have until tomorrow," Gougoutte repeated, pensive. "They told you that . . ."

We were huddled in her studio, very near the hospital. I couldn't tell if she was pleased or disappointed.

"One night," she repeated, seeming to weigh the pros and cons. "That doesn't change anything. It's too late, they're on the list."

She didn't have to spell things out: it was definitely too late to find them a hideout away from the hospital and definitely too late for one of our usual administrative shell games.

Once again we were silent. Gougoutte, perpetually smiling and cheerful, now seemed grim and worn out. And I must have looked just as done in. I had cried several times during the day, my fury mixed with despair. And yet, even at that moment, I could only think of Danielle. She was probably alone right now in her room with her big sister, wondering what was going on and feeling fear return, settle in, and grow to consume her entire being as if there were nothing else from now on.

"What if I spoke to B.?"

Gougoutte stared at me in surprise.

"To B.? But how?"

"I can call him."

"At this hour, you'll never reach him."

"Not if I call him at home."

I sprang up, suddenly full of hope, fired up.

"I'll explain to him. He's a reasonable guy, he must have children. He'll understand."

Gougoutte didn't answer, just spread open her hands in bewilderment as she watched me change back into my white coat.

"Look, Colette. I don't know . . ."

I was beyond listening to her.

It was already night when I got down to the street, with Gougoutte right behind. I crossed the main courtyard to the hospital, passed in front of the policemen without even seeing them. Nothing nor anyone could have stopped me. In a directory in the office, Gougoutte found B.'s telephone number and asked for a line.

"Come on, Colette. Are you sure?"

I shut her down with a wave of my hand.

"Who is this?"

It was a woman, her voice sounded distant and distorted by the line. A little curt and distrustful, too. That was obvious. I introduced myself, with my heart thumping.

"An intern?"

"I am an intern at the Rothschild Hospital. I have to speak with Doctor B."

Pause.

"And what do you want with him?"

"I have to speak to him. It's a case . . . It's a matter of life and death. I have to speak to him."

I began to blabber. Gougoutte stared at me, her face shrouded in the shadow of the office. There was a click, the scratching of a phone cord, the distant echo of footsteps on a wood floor. She came back on the phone.

"The doctor does not wish to speak to you."

I tried to insist, a flood of words burst forth, and then, after a bit, I realized there was no one on the line. My knuckles were white from gripping the receiver, as if I had meant to break it.

"He won't speak to me," I said, hanging up.

Gougoutte looked at me, almost as upset for me as she was for Danielle and her sister: "Colette . . ."

I was already gone, a piece of paper in my hand, where I had just written down the address of this bastard. He didn't want to speak to me, well, now he was going to see me. I was ready to scream as I crossed the grounds again, down the street, up the stairs, tearing off my white coat with the star and tossing it into a corner.

I grabbed my purse and started to leave.

"Come on, Colette . . . For starters, what are you going to say to him?"

"I'll tell him . . . I'll tell him to leave Danielle be, there!"

I turned toward her. I couldn't see for the tears.

"Don't you understand what he's doing?"

I screamed. She took my hand, but nothing in the world could calm me down.

"Yes, of course, I understand. But he's not going to listen to you. You see what he did. Come on, Colette. You know the risk you are taking."

"I don't give a damn."

I snatched my hand away, as if she were an enemy.

The rest gets lost in a fog. I took the métro, then ran down the street searching for the address. B. lived in a beautiful Parisian building. He was treating himself to a beautiful apartment with his additional pay as doctor at Drancy. The concierge let me in and I knocked on the dark wood door. I could hear the sound of footsteps, the interior smelled clean, smelled of dinner, too. In the dark, behind the door barely ajar, two narrowed eyes peered at me with suspicion.

And there I stood on the landing, demanding, begging for Doctor B. to please see me, that it was life and death, that he had to listen to me, that two innocent little girls depended on him, that we were all doctors and our duty was to save lives, that no one had the right to put Danielle on a train like that, that she was an adorable little girl, that everyone at the hospital loved her, that he would love her too if he knew her, and that even if she couldn't be helped, at least we could spare her parents from being on that train.

I exhausted myself for nothing.

The door opened a tiny bit, just enough to see those two mean eyes. Bolted shut and selfish.

"Doctor B. does not wish to see you, Mademoiselle. You have no business here. You should leave this building."

All of a sudden, I got hold of myself. The threat implicit in those words brought me to my senses. He wasn't going to see me. And if I continued to insist, they would be coming here to arrest me—with my false identity papers and no star. I looked around as if I were just now noticing where I was: the spiral staircase, the clean walls, the carpet held down with brass rods. The peaceful silence of this bourgeois apartment building. Suddenly, I was at a loss for words.

I was of no use anymore, there was nothing more to be done. Nothing. That was clear.

The door closed with a muffled click. Bitter tears poured down my cheeks as I went down into the street, drowning in sadness and disgust. And those feelings have never left me since.

The truck arrived at Rothschild at dawn.

The hospital was just waking up to a bright spring morning, as the truck made its way to the suburbs, to Drancy where the two little girls were reunited with their parents. For me, all that remains of Danielle is the memory of a child's eyes, her large inquisitive eyes, a bit apprehensive, the same look she had in a photograph taken by the intern Simon Schwartz. In it, a group of doctors and nurses are in their white coats, looking straight at the camera, four or five of them wearing the yellow star. And Danielle is in the front row, finding refuge at the foot of a tall doctor and clinging to his finger, uncertain.

And at his side, Gougoutte, all smiles. But Danielle never grew up.

The truck left, the girls disappeared. A few days later, a thousand women, men, and children, of all ages and from many countries, were loaded onto trucks and taken to the Bourget-Drancy train station, where they climbed into freight cars and were sealed in.

After two days and two nights, the doors opened on a ramp at a station in Poland, where dogs howled and well-fed young soldiers used the butts of their rifles to force them to abandon their meager bags. And while shadowy figures were already cleaning the cars, the Gradsztejn family, Danielle and Céline, their mother, Maya, and their father, Szlama, were shoved onto other trucks, a short ride to huge buildings, a factory of sorts where chimneys were belching out a nauseating stench.*

*In November 2022, a plaque commemorating Danielle and Céline Gradsztejn was unveiled at the old entrance of the Rothschild Hospital, rue Santerre.

17

Flight

I returned to the hospital unconcerned about possible reprisals. Doctor B. couldn't have cared less about me and had left no instructions concerning me. No doubt for him I was no more than a hotheaded young girl, a little stupid, who didn't understand that orders were orders.

My father didn't see things in the same way. For him my attitude was becoming suicidal.

"Come on, Colette, you can't go on like this," he said, when I told him the whole story. "What would have happened if your B. had called the police?"

I dug in my heels.

"They need me at the hospital."

"They need you alive and free. What good are you if you're arrested?"

I shrugged my shoulders. After what happened to Danielle (I considered her already dead, even if I was far from imagining how real and atrocious her death was), I was more than ever determined to fight. Enraged, filled with dreams of revenge, like a young soldier who sees his comrades die in battle. Remorse was beginning to set in too. We had to save as many children as possible, and swiftly, and stop being so naïve about it.

I went back to Rothschild like a soldier returning to the front, with fear in the pit of my stomach.

The Germans were losing, everyone knew it, they most of all. But they were still powerful and were becoming even more brutal, more merciless. Roundups at the hospital multiplied. Visitors were interrogated at the entrance and pulled aside. Men were made to drop their pants to see if they were circumcised. Then came a check of identity papers and star.

At the end of it, there was an arrest nearly every time.

In the weeks following Danielle's departure, I couldn't stop looking for her, as if a miracle would bring her back to me, as if she'd dart out from around a corner or a pavilion door. But of course the miracle did not happen. I couldn't get used to it. Sometimes, when Gougoutte looked at me, I could see that we shared the same feelings: an infinite mix of anger, sadness, impotence, the fear of not being able to finish what we were doing, the guilt of those who had survived.

The inspections came in rapid succession. Sometimes, it was a German checking the various pavilions, or a bureaucrat from the prefecture, or maybe a doctor cast in the same mold as B. We were powerless, and our hearts ached whenever we learned they had arrived: they were certain to leave with their quota of sick patients, a bitter punishment. The patients knew it, too. I saw them lie low, try to erase themselves from the world, become invisible, and pray with all their might that it not be their turn, not this time. The Nazis returned to the hospital again and again, like toxic fumes that nothing could stop. Fumes that seeped into our very beings, poisoning us all.

One day, when good weather was upon us once again, I saw a group of gawkers at the base of one of the pavilions. Others were running up to join them. The grounds were rather quiet, nothing to hear but the birds chirping, but as I approached I began to hear the murmur of the crowd.

At first, all I saw was a doctor kneeling on the ground. I could just make out part of his shoulder and a three-quarter view of his face from behind. I had a horrible premonition. As if in a dream, the circle opened to let in two nurses who came running. They threw a blanket on the ground. Then I saw a body lying there, stretched out, lifeless, one leg sticking out at a sickening angle, long hair escaping from under the blanket.

It was motionless, horrifying.

"It's a mother from the maternity ward."

My neighbor, a patient, spoke in my ear as the police in turn came running, out of breath.

"C'mon, c'mon . . . There's nothing to see here. Move along . . . Let's go . . ."

"They came to arrest her," continued the patient at my side. "Apparently, she'd just given birth. She jumped with her baby. Can you believe it?"

I had the strange feeling I was hallucinating: that long brown hair, those policemen who were gruffly pushing us back. Suddenly I recognized the one who had come to alert me when Danielle was arrested, but he was preoccupied with his horrible task and didn't see me.

"The Drancy people came to arrest her. She threw herself out the window with her kid," repeated my neighbor, as if to convince himself that it was true, that it had really happened.

I felt sick to my stomach. She had killed herself and her child, the baby she had carried for nine months and had just brought into the world, the flesh of her flesh. The blanket hid a barely visible bulge, that despite myself I knew to be the tiny body of the newborn.

I walked away in horror. The hospital no longer protected anyone. We were no longer a refuge, a hope of escape; we were a trap, a collection center for the trains.

I spent the rest of that day in a stupor, the sight of those two shattered bodies etched on my eyes.

■ Now, amid all this blackness, something else was bound to happen. And inevitably it did.

A woman had been admitted to our ward who had pretty much lost touch with reality, a Madame B.* I remember her, disoriented, scarcely knowing who she was or what she was doing there. Her story was awful: one day her husband heard a noise in the stairwell. Believing they were about to be arrested, he tried to see what was happening by sticking his head in the elevator shaft, where the elevator was usually out of order. But suddenly it started up again, and his head was crushed before her eyes. Since then she had lost her mind.

As she aimlessly wandered the streets, she got caught up in a raid and was placed at Rothschild. But she hadn't regained her reason. She barely recognized her name.

As often happened, a police inspector had just arrived on our floor. When that occurred, we always gave the patients the same warning:

"Lie flat in bed and look as sick as possible."

But for Madame B., it was a waste of breath. I'm not even sure if she still understood the significance of the yellow star that was sewn on her garment.

I stayed busy while watching the inspector, who ambled between the beds in the first ward, examining files, dates of admission and surgeries, ticking off names here, asking questions there. He then moved on toward another room, and I followed him. Suddenly my heart skipped a beat, for there was Madame B. sitting in state on her bed, in her best dress, totally involved in arranging her long hair, half smiling, as if she were primping for an evening at the theater.

Clearly she hadn't understood the warning.

My heart beat even faster, I really resented her for this. Surely she couldn't be that stupid! From some distance, I tried to signal to her: *Lie down . . . Lie down!* But she ignored me completely. The inspector was

*Germaine Blum, sister-in-law of Léon Blum, former Prime Minister of France.

heading straight toward her, down the center aisle between the two rows of beds. I tried to attract her attention, but the poor woman wouldn't stop playing with her hair, applying her makeup, smiling and perfectly at ease.

From where I was standing, I was now gesturing wildly: *Lie down, damn it! Lie down, for God's sake!* Her eyes registered my movements, but she looked right through me as she slowly and with great precision unscrewed the cap of her lipstick. I might as well have been transparent.

And so the inspector came upon her, at first surprised and then annoyed. He stopped at her bed, stood firmly planted in front of her, and then she in turn seemed to notice he was there. A long lock of gray hair fell across her face, as she looked at him confused. She seemed very calm though, with not a hint of fear.

"Madame B. is a little disoriented," Gougoutte hastened to explain to the police officer. "She needs to rest for a few days."

The inspector paid no attention to her.

"So," he said loudly to Madame B., "I see you are in good health?"

I edged closer, shaking my head in warning. *No, no, you don't feel well, you're sick. You are not ready to be discharged!* She seemed not to understand what she was supposed to do; she seemed lost, and a bit ridiculous with her bright red lips. Then suddenly she noticed me signaling and gave a start.

At that, the cop spun around while I was still signaling *No!* with my head and fingers.

A deadly silence fell over the room. He looked at me, cold as ice, and for a moment, I thought he was going to slap me there and then. His eyes took in my star, then my face. I could feel my legs start to shake.

I was caught. How stupid!

"And you are . . . ?"

"She's an intern," Gougoutte quickly intervened, as if that might protect me.

He shut her up with a murderous glance before appraising me, as a judge might examine a condemned man.

"Go wait for me in the corridor. We'll deal with this later."

With his chin he pointed to the exit. I walked out slowly, my footsteps heavy on the tile floor, then stood next to the policeman guarding the entrance. My heart was now thudding; I couldn't think. I knew this was bound to happen. I'd be taken to Drancy, put on a train.

I was admitted here as an intern, not to help Jews.

All the fears I had kept inside seemed to spew forth all at once, that terror I tried for so long to ignore. I thought about my false papers and started to shake. They would interrogate me, want to know where I lived. They would find our hideout in Neuilly.

I slumped against the wall, unable to think straight. Because of me, Papa would be arrested. It would all be my fault. Suddenly I saw Gougoutte coming. She had for a moment slipped away from the inspector's visit.

"That's it. Madame B. is being sent back to Drancy," she murmured.

I gave her an empty look. She looked surprised.

"But wait, what are you doing here?"

I pointed to the room where the inspector was making a note in his papers.

"You know . . . He told me to wait."

She shot a quick glance toward the corridor, to the policeman on guard a few steps away from us.

"And you're waiting? Run! Run now!"

As I still hesitated, she pushed me toward the corridor. Her blue eyes, normally filled with laughter, were now hard, almost mean.

"But . . ."

I pointed to the cop on duty, a few steps away. He wasn't watching us.

"But what?" she asked, pushing me toward the corridor.

And finally I got it—the cop knew nothing about the incident with Madame B. He might have seen me talking with the inspector, but maybe not. Our exchange had been very brief. And after that, he saw me come out of the room and wait in the corridor a few steps away. And that was all, nothing else.

Gougoutte made a little wave:

"Keep going!"

I took a couple of steps, then caught his eye; he gave me a quick mechanical smile before falling back into his daydream.

The stairs.

I found myself outside, my shoulders hunched, as if someone was going to call out my name and run after me. Nothing. I scurried across the hospital grounds, almost running, then through the police entrance. They waved to me. The main courtyard, the gate, Gougoutte's apartment. I felt sick to my stomach. It was impossible, they would come looking for me, or at least they would try. But no, everything was perfectly quiet. I heard children calling in the street, a car passing by. And the métro away in the distance.

Once I got to the station, everything would be better. That's if the inspector hadn't realized that I'd fled. I fumbled with the sleeves of my white coat, feverishly, with the horrible feeling that my hands had stopped listening to me. Finally, I got it off and hid it under the sheets.

I took my bag and left.

No police. Only two men chatting at the hospital entrance. I made a beeline for the Daumesnil station without looking at them, forcing myself not to run. The inspector must have realized by now; he had probably started to look for me.

But no, still nothing.

The platforms were nearly empty. It was an unusual time for me to be there, with so few passengers. Across from me a very young woman hugged a child to her side.

When the doors closed, I was still out of breath, my back soaked in sweat, my legs wobbly.

Then, with a grinding of its wheels, the train took off, heading toward freedom.

18

Mademoiselle Lecomte

I never set foot in the hospital again.

My father, who considered my flight from Rothschild both inevitable and wise, was happy I had returned to the fold. And it didn't take him long to recruit me into his Resistance organization.

I would have to have been blind not to understand the nature of his activities since his miraculous release from Drancy. I was used to seeing strangers come to the house. Some came with documents and left immediately, without saying a word; others stayed for a meal.

One evening, one of the visitors spread out a big sheet of tracing paper on the living room table. I heard him go over it for quite a while with my father, who then asked me to come take a look at it.

It was an industrial drawing that looked like a sort of big suppository, a bomb with very small fins, but of a rather novel type.

"In your opinion, is this drawing complete?" asked my father, pointing to the upper part of the contraption.

I was surprised to be asked.

"It looks like it, why? Is something missing?"

My father frowned (I still had trouble getting used to seeing him without his mustache or beard).

"We think it's missing something to propel it."

Then he went back to speculating about it with his visitor and forgot about me.

Later on I found out that these stolen plans came from Germany or Belgium. It was a V2 rocket, the precursor of the most modern ballistic missiles.

All this intelligence was sent to London, of course.

■ My enlistment was not the least bit formal. One evening, not long after I had fled from Rothschild, my father summoned me to the corner of the apartment he used as an office:

"I think you understand what I do, right?"

I nodded my head, waiting for the rest.

"Well then, I would really like you to work with me. That is, with us. Do you want to?"

I grinned.

"What do I have to do?"

"I'm going to tell you. But you know what the risks are, right?"

Of course I knew. I had seen with my own eyes what the Gestapo was capable of, and I supposed they'd really go at it if they landed on a Jew. But I had seen too much to sit back, I couldn't forgive them for what they had done to Danielle and her sister.

In vague terms, my father then explained to me that his network transmitted intelligence to London. It was essential for the Allies who were preparing the invasion of France.

"Intelligence is the heart of warfare. Without intelligence, you're operating in the dark. The more the Allies know about the Germans, the faster they'll beat them. We are their eyes and ears on the continent."

We were spies in our own country.

I had to wait until the end of the war to find out that he had used his contacts in the industrial world to recruit engineers and scientists inside the very factories that worked for the Reich. Goélette, the network he belonged to, answered directly to the BCRA,* the intelligence service of Free France.

For the moment, he didn't breathe a word of that to me. He just counseled me at length on the importance of prudence. Just as at the hospital (I had told him all about the rescue network), I was part of a group, but aside from him, my recruiter, I knew none of the other members. I had to be as careful as possible, adhere strictly to orders and nothing else.

"I'll be giving you orders and you'll have to follow them. If you are to meet someone, always be on your guard. Always arrive a little in advance, but not by too much. Take advantage of that time to check if there are people hanging around who seem to be waiting, too. If something seems out of the ordinary, don't stick around, leave. But leave calmly, like someone out for a stroll, is that understood?"

I said yes.

"Do you understand?" he repeated, looking at me like an officer testing one of his men.

I nodded my head, impressed. A new war was beginning.

▪ I had a code name: Mademoiselle Lecomte.

I was asked to memorize a surrealistic sounding code: *All herbs are salad* (*On groupe toutes les herbes sous le nom de salade*). That, it seemed, was the formality that finalized my official appointment.

But what followed was disappointing. While my dearest wish would have been to hurl bombs at the boches or machine-gun them down, I was asked instead to find the locations of anti-aircraft batteries the

---

*Created in July 1940 by General de Gaulle, the BCRA (Bureau central de renseignements et d'action) was the intelligence and operations service of Free France, often acting in concert with the British Intelligence Service, its English equivalent. It is the precursor of the current intelligence service, the DGSE (Direction Générale de la sécurité extérieure.)

Germans had installed on certain rooftops in Paris. I also had to make a note of the license numbers of all the cars I saw and describe the pennants on them, in particular those of the generals. And I had a lot on my plate: I was given the fifth and sixth arrondissements of Paris, bursting at the seams with boches, especially at the Senate and the Luxembourg Gardens, which had been transformed into a fortress.

So there I was, a bureaucratic spy.

Every morning, I took the métro to the Latin Quarter, with a book, something to eat, and whatever I needed to take notes. I spent my day there, casually mixing with crowds of students (I wasn't given this mission completely by chance). I followed my nose wherever it led, or rather, I followed it upward, trying to guess which buildings had those famous anti-aircraft guns on the roof. Most of the time, you couldn't see much from the streets, so I had to wander up the stairs on the off chance, hoping that the concierges wouldn't take too much notice of me.

Once up there, there was always an opening, a skylight, a window, or even a ladder leading to the zinc roof. From there, I could see the guns, often twin tubes aimed at the sky, jutting out from piles of bags filled with dirt. I never saw any soldiers, and that was just fine with me.

I would make a mental note of the address and walk back down, listening for sounds in the stairwell. I had a speech all prepared in case I encountered anyone: I'd come to visit a friend from school and I must have gone to the wrong building.

Apart from exploring the rooftops of Paris, my new duties allowed me to discover a bunch of things about the occupier that in general you'd be better off not knowing. I learned, for example, the meaning of the initials on their license plates: WH for army, WM for navy, SS, and so on. In the evenings, I gave all this information to my father and went off to bed, worn out.

Sometimes I was also asked to identify the places where Germans or the militia gathered; not much more interesting, but more dangerous. There were always armed guards in front, and these were suspicious times. Attacks against the occupier had become commonplace, and it was better not to seem to be preparing one.

But during these few months, fortunately, I never ran into any trouble. I must say I wasn't the only one out on the streets of Paris. The city was crawling with people on the run, people in hiding, Jews without stars, informers, and traffickers of every stripe.

For his part, my father miraculously escaped arrest, one day decamping from a locale that to him seemed suspicious. The man he was supposed to meet there was arrested and deported. Thanks to a policeman by the name of Coletta, another Resistance member, we learned later that the police were looking for my father. They had shown up at avenue Hoche, found nothing, and placed seals on the front door.

I couldn't help myself; I couldn't get the hospital off my mind.

Gougoutte, Lison, Simon Schwartz, Claire Heyman, what had become of them? Had they been arrested? Or were they continuing to smuggle children out? At times, I shuddered, imagining that the network had been discovered and that they had all been arrested and tortured.

I did everything I could to put Danielle and her family out of my mind, but the memories were too strong and came flooding back. They were like waves rushing in, one after another, each one more powerful than the last. And in these waves I heard the laughter of the little girl, I felt her fingers in my hands, I breathed in her almond scent. Yet I knew she was dead. How could it be otherwise? No deportee had ever sent news from Poland or Germany. She was my child and I had lost her. I thought too about Bijou, far from us in Belgium, and I couldn't stop my tears. In my mind, it had all become a jumble.

As the end neared, the repression worsened. The Nazis were retreating everywhere, in Russia, in Italy, crushed by the bombings. We heard about *maquis* combat, reprisals, assassination attempts.

■ Winter 1943.
Every day I wondered what good my work was accomplishing. Night after night we were awakened by bombs falling and would hear the dull thump from anti-aircraft batteries. I couldn't get used to this deafening racket. Behind the noise, I imagined dead bodies, collapsed buildings, mourning that never stopped. And yet the next day, when I climbed the stairs again, never once did I see a gun that had been destroyed. So what was my intelligence being used for?

Then spring arrived. And at last, the day we had all been waiting for.

The landings. The Germans announced they were going to push the Allies back to the sea, that the invasion would fail. But of course they would say that.

Paris had changed overnight. Although there was no significant difference in insignias and flags since the previous summer, I now saw new ones every day. It was a game of musical chairs, of officers and military units. Every day they came and they left; so many that I had trouble writing them all down. The Germans were panicked. For weeks we lived glued to the radio. The invasion seemed to be bogged down in Normandy. I feared for a time that the Germans would prevail, but no, my father was confident.

"The Americans won't let that happen. They have air superiority. Eventually, the boches will crack."

And finally crack they did. After several seemingly endless weeks, we learned that the front had been penetrated. It was one more disaster for them. I was insanely happy. Now the Germans were where we were four years earlier (such a long time ago, a whole world had changed since then): now it was their turn to withdraw in a *flexible defense* toward positions *planned in advance.* They had lost.

Our little apartment in Neuilly gradually turned into a general headquarters. (I doubt many neighbors still believed we were a peaceful Breton family that had taken refuge in Paris.) So many comings and goings of people I'd never seen before. The atmosphere became tense, like the faces of the Germans in Paris who now stared us down resentfully. The ones who had been there from the start seemed to be at the end of the road. Resigned and fatalistic, like men condemned to death.

One evening my father asked me to come into the living room, as my mother carefully watched. Two or three stick grenades were on the table, with a few others, round ones. An automatic pistol completed the tableau; it was big and black, shining, and well-oiled.

"I suppose you know what this is?" he asked.

I nodded yes. He picked up one of the stick grenades—it looked like a big hammer with white writing on the metal shell.

"Take it."

It was rather heavy and I felt incapable of ever using it, Colette who wanted to throw bombs at Germans. With grenades, you always imagined the thing exploding in your hands before you even got a chance to toss it.

"Unscrew the cap."

Once the cap at the end of the handle was off, I could see a type of porcelain ball hanging from a string.

"This is the detonator," my father explained to me, as calm as if he were talking about a nail. "You give it one hard pull and you have five seconds to throw it. And don't forget to take cover, of course."

I was far from confident while he explained to me how to take aim at the enemy with my free arm and throw the thingumajig with the other, as hard as I could. He then showed us how to handle a pistol: arming the breech, unlocking it, ejecting, and loading the cartridge. The weapon seemed to me enormously heavy, the springs awfully stiff. To tell the truth, I could not see myself using these things against human beings, but I kept my doubts to myself and disguised my dismay behind a very serious expression.

I think he knew there would be fighting and wanted to show us how to, shall we say, dissuade a possible aggressor. At the end of the lesson, I pointed out that we hadn't touched the round grenades.

He smiled at me.

"I remind you, Colette, you've never been any good at ball games. Best to avoid playing with those."

Thank God, I never had to use either the gun or the grenades.

▨ As the end approached, Papa seemed increasingly somber.

▨ "Good lord, these fools are going to get us massacred."

He was talking about the FTP, the French Communists, who dreamed of triggering an insurrection without waiting for the Americans.

"It'll end up like Warsaw: the boches will massacre us. They have tanks and troops, and what do we have? Nothing: some kids with a few pistols and grenades. . . . War isn't something you can just make up as you go along, especially against the boches."

My assignments had changed. Now I was a courier in a Paris transformed by skirmishes that bit by bit turned into urban guerrilla warfare. The city was practically deserted under a radiant sun. Sometimes you heard sporadic gunshots, followed by brutal hails of bullets, and explosions enough to take your breath away. Then a lull. Just a brief encounter. The dead and wounded were picked up. And each time, my stomach turned and I was gripped by fear.

The war was in our streets, the kind of war where the sidewalks ran with blood.

One morning very early—it was not yet six o'clock—I was walking up avenue Mac-Mahon, near the Arc de Triomphe. At daybreak, the city seemed dead. Suddenly, a civilian armed with a rifle ran across the street. Where was he going? Who knew? There was no one else around, except for me. Then, about a hundred feet away, I came across a form lying in the road. It was a horse with an enormous belly, probably killed by gunfire. When I passed by again, a few hours later, flies were swarming around the carcass; three-quarters of it had been carved off. The people of Paris were dying of fear . . . but also of hunger.

Later I passed a young couple, each on a bike. Between them they were holding a small coffin; their child's, no doubt. Funeral parlors were no longer in business. They pedaled in silence, indifferent to this absurd world.

I was often sent to the area around the Fontaine Saint-Michel, which had become one of the strategic locations for the insurrection, another being the Hôtel de Ville. People had erected barricades in a more or less organized fashion, with paving stones pulled up from the tarmac, tree grills, and piles of sandbags. Some FFI* had taken up position behind them, armed with just about anything; they seemed anxious but ready to exact revenge. We had all seen dead bodies, people burned, or shredded by shrapnel. And the Germans stayed in their holes and retaliated harshly.

Once I had to deliver a message deeper into the Latin Quarter, toward boulevard Saint-Germain. Terrifying explosions thundering between buildings made me freeze. In a second, the sidewalks emptied, passersby

---

*The French Forces of the Interior, the formal name for the French Resistance, given by de Gaulle.

threw themselves to the ground. It was impossible to see where the shots were coming from.

Near rue de Tournon, I saw a man flattened against a wall, white with fear. Between two deafening explosions, he told me that a German tank stationed in front of the Senate was raking the street with gunfire. I had to get across to deliver my message, but I felt incapable of the slightest movement. Fear had numbed my entire body. Each time a shot rang out, we all instinctively crouched down, heads hunched between our shoulders.

Another guy came over.

"I know all about tanks," he said, after another explosion. "From where he is, he can't hit anything at ground level."

But he didn't risk it and stayed where he was. Two bystanders took the plunge and got to the other side, on all fours, or crawling. It was both ridiculous and terrifying. Oh well, I had messages to pass on, so I took off without thinking.

I got up on the other side, my knees skinned, unscathed but jittery. And then I ran, my fear all but forgotten.

Except for the telephone, nothing was working: there was no métro, no electricity, no gas; all we had left to eat was a big maggot-infested smoked ham and rotting potatoes. But no one cared. At last, the Leclerc Division arrived with the Americans and it all ended in an explosion of joy. I have no words to describe what I felt: this mix of exaltation and relief, regret, remorse, this crazy happiness tainted with the shame of having survived and having been so humiliated.

■ But the war had not finished with me.

Just when I thought it was all over, I learned that I had been enlisted in the fighting French Forces for *the duration of the war*. I didn't have a choice. So there I was, decked out in an AFAT uniform, the

Army Women's Auxiliary, with the rank of chief sergeant. And I was not happy. For a year I had dreamed about throwing bombs at Germans, but they wouldn't let me. And now that the war was continuing, I was shoved into an office and made a secretary instead of being sent to the front.

Now in my fifth year of medicine, I figured I had better things to do than be a flunky in a ministry. I set about applying to join the health services. As I waited for things to sort themselves out, memories of the hospital began to eat at me. Still, I had no desire to return there, or rather, I didn't have the fortitude.

And yet I had to know. What had become of them?

I remember walking the last few meters with apprehension. More than a year had passed since I had fled, and I'd heard nothing. Anxiously, I left the métro and turned down rue Santerre. But would I have the strength to continue on inside the hospital walls? From the street, I could see the little paved courtyard, exactly as I had left it.

Only the police had disappeared from the entrance. The flags of the Allied nations had been hoisted above their loge, as if to wash away the shame of their presence.

The street shone bright in the sun. I took a few steps, trying to make up my mind. Behind the brick wall, I could make out the pavilions still intact, patients walking around, pale in the sunlight, birds singing. I was both surprised and amazed by the sense of calm.

I must have looked a bit lost in front of the entrance, neatly strapped into my brand-new khaki pea jacket with its big pockets and gold stripes on the sleeve. I didn't hear any children or any voices at all. Only people entering and leaving the hospital, taking no notice of me.

So where had they all gone? It felt strange: as if everything I had lived through had been nothing but a dream, a performance, as if everyone had left to make way for a new cast of characters who had no idea what had taken place here.

"Colette?"

It was a familiar voice.

A silhouette all in white came into the courtyard: a petite woman with laughing eyes already full of tears. It was Gougoutte, her very self, exactly as she'd always been. Suddenly I had the impression that we had only just separated. I was still in the corridor next to that stupid cop who hadn't understood that I had been arrested. I was still hearing her urging, "Run! Run now!" and feeling the pressure of her hand on my back as she pushed me toward life, toward freedom.

And we threw our arms around each other and held each other tight, two survivors.

19

Liberation

On the phone, we had a quick conversation and arranged to meet. I knew she hadn't told me everything; too much had happened, in any event. Her demeanor as she spoke made me realize that the end at the hospital had been even more horrible than I had imagined. There were no more escapes, she informed me, and this hardly surprised me. The Germans had multiplied their visits and surveillance. People had been deported, and of course no one heard from them again.

More than ever, Rothschild had become a prison.

Gougoutte stopped talking as her gaze drifted to the people walking by. Shortly after, we sat down on the terrace of a small café on boulevard de Picpus. She recounted the last months of the Occupation. So many people had vanished since the beginning. Director Halphon, Doctors Leibovici and Weismann, Jacques Ulmann, the intern with the beautiful black eyes and white streak in his hair.

Before us an elderly man passed by with a much younger woman, an infant in her arms. As we watched them, the same depressing thoughts must have crossed both our minds, of those women and children who came to Rothschild, then had to leave on the trains. No news of any of them. No news of Danielle and her family.

A maelstrom had passed over, a maelstrom of blackness and evil that had swept up everything in its path. Mademoiselle Damangout told me that when the first fighting broke out during the Liberation, the personnel was split up and sent to the different public hospitals in Paris under orders from the Resistance. The first combat wounded arrived a little later, driven by Simon Schwartz. At least he was alive.

She told me that Resistance fighters had battled the militia in the Picpus Cemetery, just behind the hospital. But I didn't give a damn about those filthy militia.

"Marie Lévy, the switchboard operator, was deported. Did you know that?"

"No, I didn't know."

"Doctor Zadoc-Kahn, too. And Marcelle Dreyfuss, the head nurse."

They had been deported, in the same trains with Jews, members of the Resistance, gypsies, homosexuals, all of them treated alike. Night and fog.*

"You know," (she pulled a face), "not everyone went along with trying to save patients."

"Yes, I know."

I was thinking of H., the head of surgery, the frightened coward who would get rid of patients before they were healed.

"There were even letters of denunciation."

I gave her a pained look.

"Who? Personnel?"

"Yes, but we don't know who. Someone was writing to the commander at Drancy. Yes, Colette, that's how it was."

I tried hard to wrap my head around that, disgusted by such stupidity and malevolence. Who could have been so contemptible as to take offense at wanting to rescue children, to spare them the trains to Germany? What difference could that have possibly made to them? I

---

*Refers to the German phrase "Nacht und Nebel." According to the German decree promulgated by Heinrich Himmler on December 7, 1941, prisoners were to be deported to camps in such a way that they would vanish without a trace, into the "night and fog."

thought about B. again, wondering what had become of him. He was probably holed up somewhere, or maybe he was hiding in plain sight, like those officers you see in operettas, those eleventh-hour "heroes" I'd seen in the last few weeks. They were the ones who spoke the loudest and acted out the most, waving their peashooters, in such a hurry to take revenge (for what—for having been so cowardly, so pathetic?) and reinvent themselves as Resistance fighters all along.

After I left the hospital, the Germans had become more and more ruthless. Dannecker, the maniac who beat up Marcel Leibovici, had been replaced by another SS brute, Alois Brunner, who was just as rabid. He rebaptized Rothschild "Camp Picpus": the hospital was just another prison. The orphanage was "Camp Lamblardie." The French police—considered too accommodating—had been replaced by guards from a private security firm. Yes, French companies got into this kind of business in 1943. Brunner would show up regularly for his inspections, with his highly polished boots and a scowl on his face. Sometimes it was mothers, sometimes old people, sometimes infants, he arrested them all. It was criminal and administrative madness. All pavilions were enclosed in barbed wire, all the non-Jews were chased out. At the end, even the new security guards were not good enough: Brunner ordered the sick prisoners to police themselves, as in the Polish ghettos. If there were escapes, prisoners and staff would be shot or deported.

Nineteen forty-four had been a terrible year for the UGIF orphanages and children's homes, up until midsummer when the American tanks were no more than a handful of kilometers from Paris. The boches wanted to destroy everything, including as many children as possible. Hundreds of poor kids were deported.

The fate of the last Jewish director of the hospital was particularly awful. Armand Kohn was one of those men with a sense of duty, hopelessly servile to authority. By meticulously obeying the Germans, he had persuaded himself that he would be spared. But of course not: he was arrested with his wife and all his children.

They were all deported just hours before Drancy, and then the hospital, were liberated.

"And Claire Heyman?"

Gougoutte sadly smiled. "The boches arrested her. But she was lucky. They had nothing on her. She was interrogated for several days and then they released her. We can go say hello, if you want. You'll see, she hasn't changed at all!"

No, surely, she hadn't changed at all. I could see her working away, exactly like before the war, saving children and helping others. She had been stronger and smarter than the Gestapo. This woman was a rock.

"But you haven't changed either! The uniform suits you well. What are you now?" she asked, pointing to my stripes. "A colonel, at least?"

I burst out laughing.

"I'm a chief sergeant, can you believe it? I enlisted in the army without realizing it. And now I have to wait till the end of the war."

I told her about my disappointments. No way I'd spend months typing up reports for some officer. I was a doctor, so I had to get into the health services and get to the front.

Gougoutte smiled broadly, all sadness gone.

"I see you haven't changed," she said, getting up. "Come on, let's go try to get a bite to eat. My treat. And you can't say no."

We walked down the boulevard for a minute, arm in arm, and then she became more serious:

"Maria Errazuriz* was also arrested," she said bitterly. "Apparently they tortured her, the ice bath."

*Yad Vashem has honored Maria Errazuriz as "Righteous Among the Nations" for helping to save Jewish children in France. In recognition of her active participation in the French Resistance, she was awarded the Légion d'honneur.

Maria Errazuriz was Claire's assistant, a Chilean woman who had helped set up the entire network. Then Gougoutte quickly reassured me, taking my hand in hers, a nurse's hand, strong and firm.

"She did fine. She didn't talk. They were forced to release her. You see, we're all still here."

She caught her breath, realizing that she had spoken too quickly. But no, I thought bitterly, we were not *all* here.

20

Pediatrician

◼ Persistence paid off and I finally obtained the rank of doctor second lieutenant, then lieutenant, but still they stubbornly refused to send me to the front where I had asked to serve. It's true, I had no experience in emergency medicine or trauma care, so it stood to reason. But it was terribly frustrating.

For a short time I was assigned to a review commission for vetting young FFI who wanted to enlist in the army, but that brought me no sense of fulfillment. They then found me another position in Courbevoie, at the old Charras barracks, which had been converted into a military hospital.

As the Allied front advanced deeper into Germany, France slowly became inundated with returning prisoners or deportees. In the spring of 1945, we learned of the unspeakable horror: the newspapers spoke of death camps, of death factories, but without actually giving any details on the special treatment of Jews.

In those camps, no one, or almost no one, had survived. Danielle . . .

The only ones who returned were prisoners or conscripted laborers of the STO,* and they were a disparate, miserable bunch. I was in charge of treating the men taken prisoner in 1940, wretched, forgotten men who

*The Service de travail obligatoire was a compulsory labor force comprising hundreds of thousands of French workers, sent to work as forced labor in Nazi Germany between June 1942 and July 1944. The STO was created by law by the Vichy government.

seemed to emerge from the dungeons of history. Captured on the roads of France in the summer of that year (many because of Pétain's deceitful words: "It is with a heavy heart that I tell you today that the fighting must cease"), they had been left to rot in captivity for more than four years, far from their families, scorned, malnourished. Many of them were in an appalling state, very weak, or suffering from tuberculosis.

To my dismay, my boss was a captain, a Dr. Mathieu,* lung specialist. But first and foremost he was an embittered Pétainist who had just been demoted, and he was having a hard time accepting that. He and his aide, both career military, were the exact opposite of our group of young officers, who had all come from the Resistance. Let's just say that the atmosphere was not the most cordial.

This pathetic idiot found nothing better to do than to impose iron discipline on these poor French prisoners, so recently liberated. He insisted on treating them as soldiers, but my God, they were just exhausted civilians, broken victims in deteriorating health, whose only wish was to go home.

As a result, he crammed sick men into barracks of ten, *in alphabetical order*, regardless of their illness. So young FFI with strep throat were thrown in with men with advanced tuberculosis, coughing out the Koch bacillus on everyone around them. It was a mean-spirited way of avenging his own disappointments but it was also criminal and sadistic, and I was furious.

Just about every day we got into this same argument.

"We have to isolate the men with tuberculosis," I said. "At least isolate them since you refuse to send them to the sanatorium."

"This is not your decision. They are soldiers and they belong to the army health services."

---

*The name has been changed.

They belong to . . .

Those words made my blood boil. They *belonged* to the health services like the Jews *belonged* to the administration at Drancy. This guy almost reminded me of B., the SOB who got Danielle and her sister deported. Well, no, these men did not *belong* to anyone, except perhaps to their families, if their families had even survived. All these thoughts crossed my mind as we glared at each other in defiance.

"At least separate them, they're going to infect everyone. Is that what you want?"

He gave me a ferocious scowl, drew himself up to his full height and stiffened, as if that would impress me. And since it didn't, that seemed to irritate him even more.

"The discussion is over, Mademoiselle."

(A cutting little remark in passing, since I was not *Mademoiselle,* but *Lieutenant.* Not that I cared, one way or the other.)

"Not for me, it isn't," I said, pursuing him down the corridor. "There are young men here being treated for strep throat. What do you want? You want them to leave here with tuberculosis?"

"If they get tuberculosis in the army, they'll get a pension."

I bit my lip to keep from swearing at him.

"And if they die of it?"

"You know the risks when you enlist in the army, Lieutenant."

"Risks are for the battlefield, not for the hospital!"

I was about ready to throw myself at him and dig my fingers into him. I was dying to insult him but that's what he was waiting for. I understood this quite suddenly when I caught the perverse glint in his eyes. But I wasn't about to give him that satisfaction.

For a few moments we stared each other down, with me a good two heads shorter than him.

"I am warning you, you'll pay for this," he finally hissed.

Without answering, I shrugged and turned on my heel. If he only knew that I didn't give a damn about his threats.

That evening I related the episode to my father. At the Liberation, he had gone back into uniform for a while and worked to get the weapons factories up and running again as the Allies advanced. He crisscrossed the country despite worsening heart problems that left him exhausted. But now he was demobilized, and I was the one who reported to the barracks every morning.

Hearing my story, he sighed heavily, a bit tired of my troubles yet totally empathetic. I had never been much of a conformist, and he knew I was not about to start now.

"OK, you're in luck. I know General Arène, the head of the health service. I'll go see what I can do for you."

A few days later, he told me that I had been granted leave in order to prepare my thesis.

My military career was over, and that was just fine with me. At last I could go back to my studies.

■ We had news of the family. Bijou was alive, alive and well. In March 1945, my mother and father made the trip to Belgium to pick her up. I remember the homecoming: I hardly recognized her. She had been gone for almost two and a half years, her features were more delicate, she was taller and thinner. She seemed on the verge of womanhood. I felt my heart beat faster and for a moment, struggling with our emotions, we stood speechless. Then she threw herself into my arms, and I felt her warmth and breathed in her scent. She held herself tight against me and a flood of images whirled through my mind: her arrival in the world, the baby bottles I used to feed her in Tunis, our walks with my friend Lucette and her little brother under a blinding African sun that painted the ground with dazzling patches of sunshine under parasol pines.

Maurice was alive too! From Tunisia, he had passed into Algeria to enlist in the French Forces. He was integrated into the American army (despite being only seventeen, like many others).

He had become an aviator and was serving on an aircraft carrier in the Pacific!

My father never saw him again. After a lightning trip to Tunisia, where Yoyo had married and had just had a baby, he returned to France, frailer than ever. He had one angina attack after another, putting his heart under great stress. And there was no effective treatment.

Then, on September 30, 1945, the moment we all knew was coming.

The world seemed as dark and gloomy as his features. He was lying down, half asleep, under a pile of blankets. His face, so proud and full of life, seemed suddenly expressionless. The doctor made it clear that there was nothing to be done. We wept a lot, and two days after that massive heart attack, my father, Samuel Brull, died at the age of sixty-five.

We buried him amid the endless gray of the Liberation.

Then as his absence began to weigh horribly on us, and my mother once again took the helm (because, like his arrest three years earlier, his death left us with no income), a ghost from the past suddenly reappeared.

The white streak in his dark hair was still there, as was his serene composure, and though his face was haggard, he had the same handsome dark eyes: Jacques.

He telephoned one day because we still had the same number. And we saw each other again.

Out of modesty we refrained from any untoward display of affection, but our eyes said it all. It was like the continuation of a conversation interrupted just the night before.

And this conversation would last the rest of our lives.

■ For hours we exchanged war stories.

His wanderings had left him with a bitter feeling of goals incomplete. After he made it to the Southern Zone, soon to be entirely occupied by the Germans, he worked for the Resistance under an assumed identity. But in early 1944, he was arrested in a roundup in Toulouse and thrown into prison without anyone knowing who he really was. What with Resistance fighters, Jews who were fleeing, traffickers, and deserters, the confusion was so great that even the Gestapo couldn't sort it all out. These *gentlemen* in their sports jackets and silk ties barely interrogated him. Subsequently, devoured by lice and bedbugs, tormented by hunger and terrified of being unmasked, Jacques spent several months in prison, first in Toulouse, then at Fort du Hâ in Bordeaux.

He was finally freed six months later, but his experiences had drained him. Having recovered now, he was being sent to Germany as a doctor with the army of occupation. I knew I would see him again.

In spite of the incredible pleasure I derived from this reunion, so full of promise, my family was once again in the same situation as at the end of 1941 when my father was interned in Drancy. His death had been a brutal blow, and the pension system was being implemented too slowly. Once again, I was alone with Bijou and my mother, with restrictions still in place, ration coupons, and their inevitable companion, the black market.

Except that we had no cash.

In truth, my mother's family in Tunisia contributed somewhat to our needs, but it wasn't enough. So I set about looking for a job. My ambition to be a pediatrician was greater than ever, but this was more pressing. I accepted the first position I was offered: employee in a clinic in Bezons, the same clinic where Dr. Destouches, better known as the fascist, anti-Semitic writer Céline, had worked before the war. I was delighted to get this position, not because of the notoriety of my disgusting predecessor but because I was in charge of medical care in the schools.

In the mornings, my client population consisted of the poverty-stricken of the area. My afternoons were devoted to the children. But soon I was up against some very uncomfortable political realities.

In this impoverished suburb, the children had suffered greatly from hunger and thirst, from all sorts of deficiencies—not to mention trauma. I received a notice from the ministry, authorizing the free distribution of milk, milk products, and various vitamin supplements for one year. All that was required of me was to identify one hundred families from among those who demonstrated the greatest need.

I did that, and I even added a few more children, because some of them were in a truly pitiful state. A few days later, my letter came back to me; it had been opened by the mayor himself who refused to send it on to the ministry. He added a very brief handwritten note:

> We cannot request or accept this assistance. We refuse to take money from those people.

From *those people* . . . What did he mean by that? I rushed into the nurse's office, furious, my violated letter in hand.

"What's this? The mayor reads my mail?"

She lowered her eyes before giving a slight nod.

"He reads all the mail. The clinic answers to the municipality."

"I disagree! What right does he have? Look, you're a nurse, aren't you? What about patient confidentiality?"

"I know. But I can't get around it. I'm a widow, and I'm not really a nurse. I don't have the diploma. If I go against him, he'll fire me."

"I don't get it. Why the hell would he care if we give milk to these kids? Has he asked the mothers what they think? Do you think they'd say no? The kids have rickets, you can count their ribs! You know that, don't you?"

She shook her head, ashamed, and then admitted to me that the mayor refused these supplements because they came from the Americans. As a good Communist, he was obeying orders from his superiors who wanted to make the American aid plan fail, at any cost. Even if that meant making children suffer.

I was suffused with anger. So he was just as stupid as all those people who let the deportations happen because orders were orders, right? Beside myself, I threatened the mayor with a complaint. He fired me but offered me seven months' salary in exchange for my silence.

I accepted, forever disgusted with politics.

I really needed that money. Jacques and I had just married and I was pregnant with our first child, André.

For a while we lived with my mother (I continued to watch over Bijou's studies, one of my father's last wishes), and then we moved in with Jacques's mother.

A year later, in 1948, we bought a practice in Noisy-le-Sec, a working-class suburb that was still half in ruins from the bombing. We set up in a rather large house in le Petit-Noisy, Jacques as a general practitioner, I as a pediatrician.

But it was a struggle to get to that point. The French Medical Association had determined that I had not taken the right courses. It was the beginning of the French national healthcare system, which didn't recognize specialists. I wanted to take care of children and nothing in the world was going to change my mind. It took me some twenty years, but in 1970, I got my credentials!

I had become a pediatrician.

I have never been bored, not even for a day. For each child contains the whole of humanity, is a world unto himself, a universe just waiting to be discovered. All that is needed is the patience of the explorer to find the right path. I am sure that this insight came to me because of Bijou. After all, I was thirteen years older, and she was frail, often sick, and I was always worried about her. There were mornings in Tunis when I didn't feel comfortable at school, like a mother going off to work and leaving a sick child. How would I find her after school? So I'd practically run home.

I have always been especially attracted to newborns. They already have reflexes, well-defined personalities that we adults have neither the subtleties nor the sensitivities to perceive. Even at eight or ten days, or a month old, they have their own lives, vulnerabilities, anxieties. It's all there right before our eyes, and we can't see it.

The pediatrician builds bridges connecting these magical beings to us, in our parent world. Some mothers know how to read the signs, like deciphering an unknown language. Others cannot, and it has nothing to do with love. It's like a gift. Some people hear music and know how to play it instinctively while others play off-key their whole lives. No one can change that. When I retired, what hurt the most was no longer having daily contact with the littlest ones.

Some mothers succeed in understanding this universe, sensing when something is not right. Others do not. But I don't judge: a mother's love can make you blind, more surely than any other kind of love.

One of my greatest scares as a mother occurred one morning when my son André came and pulled on my sleeve.

"Maman, come look, it's funny, my pee-pee is red."

I raced to the bathroom and saw traces of red around the edges of the toilet bowl. My eyes were bulging, my mouth went dry. His urine was red, he had kidney cancer. He was going to die.

With a lump in my throat, I called a friend of mine, a pediatrician. How could this terrible thing be happening to me? What were we going to do, where should we go for treatment?

"So how long has André's urine been red?" asked my friend.

"How long . . . ?"

I could hardly speak. My panicked thoughts were all over the place.

"Since . . . since this morning. Yes, this morning."

A pause.

"Did you do a stool analysis?"

A microscopic analysis. That's what I would have immediately ordered for any of my patients. But not for André. I had flushed the toilet without thinking, as if that would get rid of the blood in his urine.

"No. It happened this morning."

Another pause. I thought she was already thinking about the best hospital, the best specialist. And I was thinking about what I would say to Jacques, the words I was going to have to find. About treatments. About how we were going to manage and the suffering we would have to endure.

"What did you eat last night?"

The question threw me, and I had to think about it, but I finally came up with the menu. Why would that matter?

"And the main course?"

"Some . . ."

And then I started to laugh, as relieved as a condemned man who has just been pardoned. We'd had beets, and that's why the Brull-Ulmann family pee-pee was red. In a second, the panicked mother had forgotten seven years of medical school and almost as many in the practice of pediatrics.

▪ After André, we had two more children: Elisabeth in 1949, and Annette, some years later, in 1955, because I had always wanted three children.

But there was always this weight within me, the weight of the horrors I had witnessed and above all the unshakeable burden of remorse. Over time I had persuaded myself that silence could erase the bad memories. But that proved to be untrue. The grief just kept circling around, like a prisoner in a cell: pounding on the bars, marking time in the darkness, and returning as soon as you are alone with yourself.

Danielle's disappearance haunted me every day. Every day I'd see her in my thoughts, I'd hear her voice and her laughter, her quick step. I could almost smell her. Then suddenly she was gone, wrenched away by B. I couldn't move, I was powerless, my hands outstretched in a silent cry. Then the vision would abruptly vanish and I'd be left with my remorse.

When my children were teenagers, they wanted to know. They knew that Jacques and I had participated in acts of resistance during the war. So we finally told them, in bits. To be honest, I spoke as little as possible. I blamed myself for having survived while Danielle had died such a horrible death along with so many others.

Eventually I heard about the work of Serge and Beate Klarsfeld. In the 1980s I learned in particular that they were pursuing a man whose name brought back the horror: Alois Brunner, the former commander at Drancy, the Nazi who had replaced Dannecker. It was too late to do anything in Dannecker's case; he had committed suicide in Germany at the end of the war. But Brunner, his successor, had survived and taken refuge in Syria; the Klarsfelds were trying to get him extradited.

Brunner had exhibited a maniacal energy. He had carried out round-ups in orphanages, in hotels, on trains, on the Riviera in the former Italian zone. He sent dozens, hundreds of children to their death.

Yet so many others had been saved. I had to tell the story. I had to chase away my shame and my regrets. I had to talk.

Little by little, I set about recalling what we had done under Claire Heyman's direction. I could see her face, so clear and yet so distant. Memories long buried began to resurface. And I told myself that these were good memories. That I didn't have the right to silence them. They were there, ready to be spoken. In my mind, Claire was once again approaching me out on a hospital path, saying:

"I have a job for you. We have to get some children out."

And I heard myself answering:

"When? What do I have to do?"

I thought back to that one rescue I remembered in detail, with the little boy heavy on my arm and the little girl walking valiantly beside me, so quiet. I remembered the door that opened to swallow them up in the night, leading them into the anonymity that would give them life and freedom.

I had to speak. And so, I spoke.

I described the hospital, the great summer roundup of 1942, the elderly who were dying, the children who ran around on the hospital grounds. Those who had been afraid and those who had been brave: Claire Heyman, Gougoutte, Schwartz, and the others.

But I never spoke about Danielle and Céline. I still couldn't. It was beyond my strength, my courage, my sense of decency.

I know this seems stupid, but I couldn't do it. That's how it was.

■ The years passed. André, Elisabeth, and Annette all had their own children. My grandchildren. They too grew up, and they too asked questions. They knew that Colette had *done something*. I told them about the hospital, but never about Danielle. And they kept insisting, as if they knew I had a secret.

And then finally I told them.

Danielle and Céline, so beautiful, so pure, carried away in cattle cars and snuffed out like two bugs. It was hard to get the words out. As I spoke, I felt like I was locked in the train with them, with the smell, the hunger, and the suffering, the suffering of knowing that it would not end, that there would never be respite or relief.

And even now that I have told the story, I still cannot bear it. I cannot bear it and I cannot understand it.

21

After

A short time after the war, we were summoned to testify against Doctor B., the bastard who had the little girls deported.

Facing judgment, he held his head high and defended himself methodically, with the callous bad faith of someone who feels neither remorse nor regret. The trains? Yes, yes, of course he knew about them, but he didn't know where they were going. And how could he have known, since no one knew?

"They were cattle cars. We knew that the conditions were harsh. But we didn't know about the rest. If we had known . . ."

How do you respond to that? Besides, what would he have done had he known?

I wanted to shout that question to him from across the room.

"The kids were not ill. There was no reason for them to be at the hospital. I followed orders, didn't I? I did my job as a doctor."

"That's true. But you were already a doctor in the public hospital system. Why did you take this job at Drancy?"

"I just took it. It was a job as a doctor. I didn't know."

"But you knew it wasn't just any doctor's job, didn't you? You knew what Drancy was being used for, isn't that right?"

"No more than anyone else. I was offered the job and I took it."

They were going around in circles. He knew it, and he took advantage of it. What he should have said, and this is the sad truth, was that nothing had forced him to work in the infirmary at Drancy. He did it for a bit of money, a bit of power. Or maybe he didn't think it was so bad, all those Jews piled on top of each other in filth, starving, terrified, maybe he was rather pleased to see them leave at dawn on their trains. Maybe he liked it. He liked humiliating. He liked using all the power he had to crush a little girl of three.

And to deport her on a train without batting an eyelash. Because orders are orders. It was all repugnant, disgusting, pathetic. He was a bastard, a miserable, run-of-the-mill bastard, with no redeeming qualities. But there are no laws against that.

B. was found guilty: three months' suspension.

I preferred to forget him, let him go to hell. And anyway, that wasn't going to bring anyone back.

■ Over time I found out what had happened to everyone whose paths crossed mine at the hospital.

Most had survived. First of all, Claire Heyman, indomitable and silent. A few days after the Liberation, she was back in her little social worker's office, once again filling out her questionnaires and forms, finding homes for children. But this time there was no more risk of death. Many of the children she saved wrote or came to see her, calling her Aunt Claire. Everyone was aware of the role she had played, but she never talked about it. Nor did she ever write anything about this time, and so the veil she cast over her network has never been lifted. No historian will ever unravel the complicated threads of her underground network.

Claire Heyman lived only for her work and for others. She never married and continued in her job as social worker until she retired. Illness caught up with her at the end of her life, a tragic affliction that wipes out your memory, so cruel. Some people who saw her in those days said that sometimes she'd cry out in the hallway:

"Run, run, you're going to be arrested!"

She passed away in the late 1990s.

I often saw Gougoutte, who also devoted her life to the hospital. To the end, she kept those same blue eyes, innocent and full of laughter, her same good humor, and her absolute devotion to others. She lived to be very old, and I was with her when she died. As I left her, I realized how exceptional she and the women of Rothschild had been. I learned that Maria Errazuriz had spent a part of her great fortune helping the children, then finally returned to her native Chile and never came back.

For a long time I continued to see my accomplices from the lab, Lison and Hirsch-Marie, Mademoiselle Damangout, Claire Heyman's little soldiers. The others—Simon Schwartz, Weissman, Lobelsohn, Perel, Dupont—I lost sight of them. I was working hard and raising my own children.

Father Kenneth had also survived. We corresponded for a while. One day, he told me he would be going back to his monastery and I never heard from him again. Like Claire Heyman, he had done his duty and was returning to civilian life just like the Roman citizens of old, who went back to tilling their fields once war was over.

In 1945, my father, who had already been awarded one Croix de Guerre during the Great War, received another for this one. He was named Officer of the Légion d'honneur, posthumously. I too received the Croix de Guerre with distinctions, awarded by General de Gaulle, as well as a letter from the American authorities acknowledging my service treating Allied aviators. These awards remained shut up in a closet and I never spoke about them to anyone.

As I said, Dannecker, the first commander at Drancy, committed suicide; this was after his arrest by the Americans. He was one of the main actors responsible for the extermination of European Jews. Brunner died in Syria, after avoiding several assassination attempts by both the French and the Israelis. He always regretted not killing more Jews.

Samy Halfon, the first director of the Rothschild Hospital, managed to escape from the camp at Compiègne, where he had been incarcerated after Drancy. He joined the Maquis and fought with them until the war ended.

Leibo survived until the Liberation by hiding here and there, in almost complete destitution.

The great Doctor Worms, who is perhaps the one holding Danielle by the hand in the photo, wound up fleeing the hospital, which had become a trap. He joined the Free French Forces in Algeria, then later participated in the Italian campaign in the army of General de Lattre.

▪ I need to come back to B.

Toward the end of the 1970s, I learned there were doctors at Tenon Hospital in Paris (where sick Jews were interned before Rothschild) who refused to address a certain professor. He *hadn't been correct* during the war. A collaborator. A self-important doctor, a big shot whose career in the public hospitals of Paris had never seen a setback. Well, almost never.

After going to ground God knows where in the immediate aftermath of the war, B. got his judgment reviewed two years later—careful this time not to have us testify. Only a few handpicked friends were summoned. He was cleared, reinstated as hospital doctor, and ended his career as professor of medicine. He was a brilliant man, no doubt about it.

Despite the disparaging attitude of certain doctors toward him, he was in no hurry to relinquish his position at retirement age. He received an extension—an exceptional extension, for *war deeds*. What these were, no one ever knew. Just like no one ever knew how this character managed to obtain the Légion d'honneur.

Which he wore proudly, it seems, on his lapel.

▨ But maybe this was our fault, after all.

While Claire Heyman continued to go to work each morning at her little office at Rothschild, now a public hospital,* and while I was caring for children in my practice, B. took his own sweet time weaving together his network, building brick by brick the story of an exemplary member of the Resistance. He had worked out his little schemes, arguments he would use when he asked for the review, contacts he could call on, his make-believe war, *his war deeds*.

And we kept our silence. As if our network had never existed. As if no child had been saved.

Little by little, the witnesses passed on. Claire Heyman first, then Gougoutte. Yet children had been saved. They could not tell their story, but they were there, they were living.

They were meant to die, but they were very much alive.

It was for them that I began to bear witness. Not only to my children and grandchildren, but to others. I needed to tell people who Claire was, who Mademoiselle Damangout was, who the children were, those passing shadows that disappeared. I had to tell the story of the little girl in the photograph, who Danielle and Céline were, and identify the bastard who sent them to their death.

I wasn't speaking for myself, but for the others.

There were commemorations, exhibitions. A plaque on the front wall of the hospital. There were a few articles in the media and a documen-

---

*In 1954, the Rothschild family sold the Rothschild Hospital to Assistance Publique–Hôpitaux de Paris, the public hospital system of Paris, for one franc.

tary on television. I have become the sole, the last survivor, and tirelessly I have repeated the story of Claire and the children she saved, always the same story, without ever forgetting those two little girls, without ever forgetting that bastard.

I know it's a bit late. We should have questioned Claire, urged her to tell everything she knew, have her search her memory for the names she could recall, the names of the Catholics, the Jews, the Protestants, the knowns and the unknowns, the names of the children and the adults who took part in the rescues, to hear their stories. This should have been done, but it wasn't.

But all the same, their story will not be forgotten.

One day I learned the truth about Danielle's fate.

I had to bring her photo to the office of Serge Klarsfeld, who at that time was collecting photographs of all the deported children for his organization, and there I was welcomed by a woman of about seventy. When I explained to her who the little girl was, her face froze. She turned pale and her lips began to tremble.

"I know Danielle," she said to me. "I know Danielle and Céline. They were my cousins."

I felt like I'd been punched in the stomach. This woman was around the same age the two little ones would have been had they survived. We sat down somewhere so she could tell me the story.

"My parents very quickly understood that we had to hide. They were both Polish Jews. Papa was a high-end furrier for the big fashion houses. When they started arresting men, he decided to go into hiding. At night he would sleep in his studio. He was fearful for us as well and, thanks to a couple in our building, he found a family in the Sarthe to take us in, my brother and me. My mother also ended up in hiding. But my aunt, the mother of Danielle and Céline, refused to let them go."

"You think they could have gone with you?"

"I believe so. Even later, when Danielle and her sister were at Rothschild. In October 1942, my brother and I came back to Paris for a few days. My father took us to a photographer and Danielle was there; she'd been sneaked out of the hospital to have a photograph taken."

As she spoke, the world around us faded away. In an instant, I went back sixty years, back to the hospital with its red brick pavilions, the garden grounds. I could see Danielle again, playing and running with her sister. I was with her, taking her home to eat with my family, and I could hear her asking me her funny, innocent questions.

Danielle's cousin spent the end of the war with her brother in a village in the Loiret. Their mother also was in hiding and their father was supposed to join her. But the concierge denounced him, and he was arrested and deported in February 1944.

"Maman never recovered. She was wracked with grief. Every day, she went to the Hôtel Lutétia* for news of the deportees, my father, of course, but also Danielle, Céline, and their parents. 'Dear God, bring them back.' But of course no one ever returned. It was so hard. . . ."

She stopped talking as a wave of sadness swept over her face, though she tried to replace it with a smile. I could picture her devastated childhood, amid a procession of ghosts. Her cousin Danielle led the procession, walking so slowly that finally she moved no more, frozen forever in her memory.

In the 1970s she met Serge Klarsfeld and began to work for him in his organization, the Sons and Daughters of the Jewish Deportees of

---

*After the liberation of Paris in August 1944, the Hôtel Lutétia, which had been occupied by the Abwehr, the German counterintelligence services, became a repatriation center for displaced persons, prisoners of war, and returnees from concentration camps. There they were registered, given clothing, identity cards, ration books, money, and a bed. Families searching for their loved ones posted missing-person notices and photographs on the walls, and wandered around showing snapshots to survivors.

France. That had helped her to mourn and free herself somewhat from the weight of the dead.

And now I knew the horrible truth.

Danielle and her sister had had freedom at their fingertips. Early on, they could have left for the Creuse or the Sarthe like their cousins, to the same farms. And later, they might have left the hospital, smuggled out through Claire Heyman's network. It is impossible that Claire never suggested it to their parents.

She must have insisted, and probably so did Gougoutte, who had a special pass for Drancy. Undoubtedly they both would have made every effort to convince the parents that their daughters would be better off away from the hospital, that there was a possibility of getting them out.

Gougoutte might have said: "Danielle and Céline are not safe with us. They can be arrested at any time and forced to return here, to Drancy, and we won't be able to do anything about it. We have to get them out, do you understand? We can take care of everything. We will deal with everything concerning the papers, you won't have any trouble with Drancy." Or so I imagined.

"But my aunt never agreed," her cousin said again. "She did not want to be separated from her daughters. They all died the day they arrived there, in June 1943. . . ."

There was nothing more to say.

A world of regret united us, unexpected companions in suffering.

I have always told myself that we could have saved them, that we should have saved them. I am unable to think otherwise, even though I know that we could not have acted without the parents' authorization. Without their consent, it was impossible. I could not have acted on my own, the entire network would have been blown. I know all that, but that's how it is, the remorse is always there.

So that's how it is, things happen, and nothing and no one can stop them.

I became a caregiver in my effort to push back against those terrible moments when man is helpless against evil.

This struggle has lasted all my life. As a pediatrician, I have seen children succumb to sickness, I have been powerless and as mad and angry with my powerlessness as I had been in the courtyard of the hospital. But I have cared for and healed other children. And when an illness was in retreat, when it gave up the fight just before fleeing, the children would look at me, exhausted, weak, but happy and alive.

And they would smile.

Those smiles, those faces have given light to my life, they have helped heal my wounds, and they have joined with those of Danielle and Céline, my three children, and all the others in a dance to life and to love.

The Network

▧ No historical work has been written on the network in the Rothschild Hospital because its principal leaders, starting with Claire Heyman, left no written documentation. In 2011, a commemorative plaque was placed at the entrance of the Rothschild Foundation, rue de Picpus, in Paris. Here is the text in its entirety as it appears on the plaque:

The Rothschild Foundation

From 1941 to 1944,
The Establishments of the Rothschild Foundation:
The Hospital, the Orphanage, the Old People's Home, the Sanitorium,
Portions of which were requisitioned by the Vichy police,
Were transformed into an annex of Camp Drancy.
During this period,
The blackest of its existence,
Certain members of the personnel of
The Foundation acted with great heroism.
They contributed to saving the lives
Of many children and adults who,
Because they were born Jewish,
Were promised certain death
In the Nazi extermination camps.

We express our gratitude to them.
They are an honor to our Foundation.

Among them,
Leading The Network of Resistance and Rescue
At the Rothschild Foundation

Maria ERRAZURIZ and Claire HEYMAN
Social Workers

Samy HALFON, Dr. Léon BONAFÉ
Directors

Dr. ASTRUC, Dr. BIRMAN, Dr. Léon ZADOC-KAHN (deported)
Dr. Jean WEISSMANN, Dr. Marcel LEIBOVICI
Dr. Robert WORMS, Dr. Colette BRULL-ULMANN
Doctors

Violette TRIVIDIC, Germaine MARX, Georgette WEILL
Nurses

Fanny JELIKOVERE (deported), Mary LÉVY (deported)
Telephone Receptionists

Annie ASSOU, Désirée DAMENGOUT, Marcelle DREYFUS (deported)
Head Nurses

Yvette WORMS
Bursar

Pierre MONIN
Head Electrician

May their courage serve as an example to future generations.